LEADING AFTER THE STORM

How to Communicate, Calm, and Coordinate in the Wake of Disaster

DR. KARISSA THOMAS

Leading After the Storm
How to Communicate, Calm, and Coordinate in the Wake of Disaster

Published by Efficient Adjuster Publishing
www.efficientadjuster.net
Printed in the United States of America

ISBN 978-1-968277-17-8

Interior Design: Marigold Emal

This book is a work of nonfiction. The insights, tools, and stories reflect the author's personal experience, professional expertise, and publicly available research. Every effort has been made to ensure accuracy at the time of publication.

For bulk orders, speaking engagements, or licensing inquiries, contact:
drk@drkarissathomas.com

Library of Congress Control Number: 2025912441

Dedication

For those who stood when the ground gave way,
who stayed when the world looked elsewhere,
and who rebuilt not only what was lost, but what was possible.

In remembrance of lives forever shaped by disaster—
from the towers that fell on 9/11 to the fractured streets of Port-au-Prince,
from the waters that swept Kerala to the winds that shattered New Orleans,
from the waves of the Indian Ocean to the global shadow of COVID-19,
and to every unseen crisis that redrew the map of human endurance.
This book honors the unseen architecture of recovery—
the leaders without titles,
the helpers without applause,
and the communities whose quiet strength carries the world forward.

THE STEADY GROUND MANIFESTO
For Anyone Called to Respond When the World Shifts

When tragedy strikes, and the systems you relied on fall silent,
You are still here.
And that means something.

You do not need a title to lead.
You do not need a microphone to make impact.
You only need presence, courage, and a steady return to what matters.

Let this be your anchor:

Breathe before you act.
Inhale calm. Exhale chaos. Let your breath remind your body
that you are safe enough to begin.

Name what is real.
Pain. Confusion. Disorientation. Hope.
Name them without shame—what is named can be processed.
What is hidden will lead.

Choose presence over perfection.
You are not expected to fix everything.
You are invited to show up fully—with honesty, compassion, and
humanity.

Be the steady one.
The one who holds a gaze.
The one who listens longer.
The one who steadies others simply by staying grounded.

Protect what matters.
People. Dignity. Memory. Kindness.
In urgency, protect the soul of the situation—not just the structure.

Take one step toward care.
Offer water. Share silence. Ask someone's name.
You do not need a full plan to be helpful—just a full heart.

Let grace find you.
You will not do it all perfectly.
But if you keep showing up with truth, care, and courage—
You are leading.

You are not alone.
You are not failing.
You are not forgotten.
You are the steady ground.

—Dr. Karissa Thomas

Acknowledgments

To the communities who showed me the truest form of leadership—not in titles, but in the quiet steadiness during a crisis. Your courage, clarity, and care have become my teachers.

To every educator, adjuster, NGO worker, elder, counselor, principal, responder, and volunteer who stood in the gap when systems faltered—these pages carry your unseen stories. You are the architects of recovery the world too often overlooks.

To the frontline leaders in the Philippines, South Africa, India, Haiti, California, Puerto Rico, and beyond—your steady hands and quiet hearts remind us all that true strength does not shout; it endures.

To my mentors and collaborators across countries, cultures, and disciplines—thank you for broadening my understanding of what leadership requires in times of upheaval. Your wisdom shaped both the work and the worker.

To my global team, who carried pieces of this book across time zones, languages, and long nights—your unseen labor helped keep the vision steady when the weight grew heavy.

And to you, the reader—

Thank you for being the kind of leader who rises not for recognition, but because the moment calls.

Your presence matters more than you know.

Disclaimer

This book is a leadership guide based on lived experience, field observation, and emotional intelligence frameworks. It is not intended to replace official emergency response protocols, legal advice, clinical guidance, or institution-specific training.

While the stories, tools, and strategies shared in these pages are drawn from real-world events across diverse cultural and geographic contexts, they are not exhaustive. Every disaster is unique, and effective response requires sensitivity to local laws, traditions, infrastructures, and needs.

Readers are encouraged to adapt the insights presented here in collaboration with community leaders, medical professionals, government agencies, and cultural stakeholders. The author and publisher disclaim any liability for actions taken based solely on this material, and recommend seeking appropriate guidance when responding to any emergency or crisis event.

Contents

Read This First: For the One Leading in Loss

There are storms that tear through our lives without warning—leaving no time to prepare, no space to breathe, and no clear path ahead. But this storm did not come to destroy me. Even when it cracked my foundations and stole the breath from my lungs, even when it shattered the version of life I thought would last—it came not just to break, but to reveal. In its wake, I uncovered truths I had buried. I saw what was fragile. I touched what was sacred. And I learned that grief, when honored, becomes a teacher.

I am not the same person who walked into the storm. I am quieter now—yet not weaker. There is a stillness inside me I didn't have before, a clarity that only comes from watching everything fall apart and choosing to rebuild anyway. I don't fill silence just to prove I am still standing. I listen longer. I speak with care. I no longer lead from urgency or image. I lead from presence. From steadiness. From the kind of strength forged in darkness and shaped by fire.

Pain does not simply vanish. But it can be transformed. Grief can stretch our capacity to hold others. Loss can teach us to become more honest, more tender, more awake. Even disaster, with all its devastation, carries within it a strange possibility—the possibility of redesigning what we build, how we show up, and who we choose to become. I will not waste this storm. I will not pretend it did not change me.

Instead, I will repurpose its ruin into roots—roots that ground me in compassion and nourish my leadership with deeper truth. I will remember that healing is not always loud, and strength does not always roar. I will become a living reminder to those around me: you are not alone in your ache. And you are not broken beyond repair.

This is not a return. This is a reconstruction. A deliberate rising into something wiser, softer, and more whole. I lead after the storm not because I was spared from it, but because I survived it. And survival carries responsibility. Now, I choose to build again. To build with empathy. To build with wisdom. To build with vision born of fire and hope shaped by loss.

If I am still here, then there is still work to do. Still stories to tell. Still light to bring. And from that truth, I will lead.

Personal Reflection: The Weight of the Storm

Holding Steady When Others Are Watching

I remember exactly where I was when the planes crashed into the Twin Towers. I was a freshman in college, on my way to class, when the television screens stunned us into disbelief. What I was seeing did not feel real — not at first. My college campus was less than an hour from New York City. Close enough to feel its pulse, yet far enough for us to stand motionless as the images unfolded before us. Everyone was ready to take action, but no one quite knew what to do. The instinct within you urges you to act, to help, to respond — yet sometimes you find yourself frozen, caught between urgency and uncertainty.

I remember desperately trying to call family members who lived in New York City, but every call failed. The lines were overwhelmed, and silence met me on the other end. That silence carried its own kind of fear — the fear of not knowing if your loved ones were safe, and having no way to reach them. In that moment, as in many moments since, I learned that helplessness is its own kind of storm.

Years before, I had found myself face to face with the power of nature. I was on a camping trip, surrounded by the beauty of the outdoors, when I waded into a river with others. The water was stronger than it appeared. The current caught me, pulling me swiftly into its grip. I remember the terrifying sensation of being swept away, powerless to stop what was happening. My feet lost contact with the ground. The river was not malicious, but it was indifferent to my struggle. Had it not been for one of the adult chaperones who saw me and reached out, steadying me and pulling me from the current, the outcome could have been very different. Sometimes, the saving hand of another is what allows us to survive the storm.

Years later, I found myself once again caught in the middle of the unexpected—this time while living in Saudi Arabia. I was dining in a restaurant when a fire suddenly broke out. There were no alarms, just smoke rising—quiet at first, then unmistakable. People began to panic. We didn't speak the local language, and no official instructions came. All we could do was make educated guesses and follow the crowd's movement. We raced down flights of stairs with strangers, each of us moving quickly yet uncertainly, driven by instinct and hope.

It wasn't the first time I had found myself running down stairs to escape the unknown. Years earlier, I had done the same in my Manhattan high-rise during a citywide emergency. I remember the metallic echo of hundreds of feet pounding down the narrow stairwell, the stale air thick with anxiety and sweat. Every few steps, someone would turn and glance behind them—not out of paranoia, but for reassurance, as if eye contact alone could steady the nerves. There were no elevators, no announcements, just an unspoken understanding that we had to keep moving. Fear traveled silently, carried between strangers like static in the air.

And then again, another day, another crisis—this time inside Macy's Herald Square. Nine flights down, shoulder to shoulder with strangers, escalators shut down, elevators frozen. The luxury of convenience replaced by the urgency of escape. Shoppers who had just been browsing for perfumes or handbags were now gripping handrails and holding their breath, the weight of uncertainty pressing in like the heat of too many bodies in close quarters. Every step down was a mix of hope and calculation—*Is this the right decision? Are we going fast enough? Is this really happening?*

In both moments, I remember how desperately we scanned one another's faces—not to assign blame or look for answers, but to find steadiness in someone else's eyes. In crisis, reassurance often comes not from experts or officials, but from the person beside you—the woman clutching her child, the man quietly helping an elder navigate the stairs, the stranger who whispers, *"It's okay, we've got this."* That's the hidden fabric of humanity we rarely speak about: the micro-moments of leadership that rise when the world starts to fall apart.

The speed at which a calm moment can unravel is always startling. In that chaos, I learned again that crisis does not always come with a warning—but it always calls for presence.

I am not unique in this experience. So many of us have lived through quiet moments that turned suddenly, forcing us to navigate personal storms that often go unseen by the rest of the world. And now, in an era shaped by digital media, even private moments of crisis can feel amplified, as images and stories spread instantly across platforms, deepening the emotional imprint these events leave behind.

As I grew older and stepped into my role as an educator, I encountered crisis again — this time not from nature, but within the walls of a school. I remember being placed in lockdowns for various reasons. In those moments, my heart pounded and my mind raced, but I could not afford to show it. The students were watching. The staff was watching. You become the calm they need to see. Even as the storm rages inside, your steady presence becomes their anchor.

Crisis does not always announce itself. It arrives suddenly, without warning. It tests not only our plans but also our poise. And yet, leadership in those moments is not about having all the answers. It is about being the steady hand, the clear voice, and the calm presence when others cannot find their footing.

That is why I wrote this book — to give voice to what it means to lead after the storm has come. To honor those who step forward — sometimes while trembling — and create emotional safety for others in the aftermath. This is not theoretical leadership; this is leadership in real life, where decisions are made while hearts are pounding, where clarity is rare, and where lives often hang in the balance.

How to Use This Book

Having worked directly alongside leaders across education, government ministries, humanitarian agencies, and corporate sectors throughout the Middle East, North America, Africa, Asia, and beyond, I have witnessed how emotional steadiness and cultural fluency transcend borders. The leadership frameworks presented here are not theoretical—they are drawn from lived experience, field observation, and real-time leadership across diverse global contexts where crisis and recovery intersect.

Leading After the Storm is not a manual confined to a single profession or moment. It is a human-centered leadership guide designed to travel with you—into classrooms, coordination centers, policy summits, NGO field operations, government briefings, faith-based spaces, and the private moments where decisions are made without certainty.

The chapters are intentionally designed to remain adaptable, applicable, and alive across multiple leadership settings. Here are several ways you may engage with this work:

1. Education-Based Leadership Development

Chapters 4, 8, 10, 11, 12, and 17 offer essential grounding for educators, administrators, counselors, and school leadership teams navigating crisis recovery within disrupted learning environments. Use these chapters to guide professional development workshops, trauma-informed leadership sessions, and school-wide conversations on emotional safety and resilience after upheaval.

2. Government, NGO, and Humanitarian Team Onboarding

Parts I and III introduce core leadership frameworks for government responders, cross-sector teams, and NGO staff entering high-pressure coordination roles. These chapters can be paired with simulation exercises, intercultural briefings, and disaster response training modules to equip staff with emotional steadiness and cultural humility in the field.

3. Community Leader Retreats and Grassroots Leadership Workshops

Use each section of the book to facilitate multi-session conversations with grassroots leaders—faith leaders, youth advocates, elder councils, volunteer organizers, and shelter coordinators. Invite participants to surface their own lived leadership experiences and co-create recovery wisdom rooted in local knowledge and collective care.

4. Post-Disaster Team Debriefs and Resilience Check-Ins

Chapters 10, 11, 12, and 17—along with the Appendices—offer practical tools for addressing emotional fatigue, preventing burnout, and recalibrating team energy during extended deployments or prolonged recovery phases. Use these reflection tools in staff check-ins, field team resets, and leadership renewal sessions.

5. Cross-Cultural Leadership Training and Global Capacity Building

Chapters 7, 9, and 16 serve as essential entry points for leaders operating across language, history, identity, and cultural complexity. These chapters can anchor cross-cultural leadership programs, humanitarian diplomacy training, and trauma-informed global leadership development.

Global Field Use and Multi-Sector Training Adaptability

This book was written as a globally adaptable resource for leaders across multiple disciplines and sectors. The vignettes, leadership tools, and applied frameworks may be integrated into:

- Government ministries, disaster response agencies, and inter-agency leadership teams
- International NGOs, humanitarian relief organizations, and global development agencies
- K-12 schools, higher education leadership programs, and trauma-informed education cohorts
- Corporate leadership, crisis management, risk mitigation, and global workforce wellness teams
- Faith-based organizations, nonprofit networks, community coalitions, and grassroots leadership alliances

Leading After the Storm may also serve as a core or supplemental text for graduate-level study in:

- Disaster Leadership and Emergency Management
- Humanitarian Studies and Global Public Administration
- Trauma-Informed Education and Community Resilience
- Nonprofit Leadership and Intercultural Management

The content is adaptable for staff onboarding, disaster certification programs, leadership retreats, cross-cultural training institutes, and localized leadership development initiatives worldwide.

Licensing, Institutional Use, and Custom Training Partnerships

Portions of this book may be licensed for institutional training, curriculum development, cross-cultural leadership certification, or formal organizational use. For licensing inquiries, institutional adoptions, or custom leadership collaborations, contact:

drk@drkarissathomas.com

Preface

This book reflects lessons drawn from disaster leadership patterns observed across more than a dozen global regions—including North America, Latin America, Sub-Saharan Africa, the Caribbean, South Asia, East Asia, Southeast Asia, the Gulf States, Central Asia, the Arctic Circle, Europe, and the Pacific. The case examples reflect lived experiences of educators, healthcare teams, NGO responders, faith leaders, grassroots organizers, and community leaders who carry the emotional and structural weight of recovery long after crises fade from global headlines.

I did not write this book based on theory. I wrote it from the heart of the chaos—from conversations with leaders who had no backup plan, from the silence that followed the departure of emergency teams, and from the emotional exhaustion that arises after holding everyone else together. I wrote it for those who do not wait to be appointed but step forward because the moment demands it. I wrote it because we are living in an age of continuous upheaval, and the world keeps looking to people like you to help keep it steady.

Disasters come in various forms: floods, fires, earthquakes, system failures, political unrest, and pandemics. Sometimes they appear overnight, while at other times they develop slowly, ultimately overwhelming a community from within. In each of these instances, someone must rise—not to control the chaos, but to coordinate care. Not to fix what is broken, but to foster a sense of order when everything seems to be unraveling.

Even in 2025, the world continues to remind us how urgently these leadership principles matter—from wildfires in Canada to aviation disasters, including the 2025 India plane crash that claimed over

279 lives and captured global attention; from global conflicts to quiet, unseen crises that rarely make headlines. The need for steady leadership remains as essential as ever.

That person is often not a government official or a crisis manager. It may be a school principal, a volunteer, a neighborhood elder, a nurse, or a teenager with a clipboard and a steady voice. It is someone who is affected but still willing to take action. Someone who cares deeply enough to lead without having all the answers. Someone like you.

Whether you are leading a village response team, managing a shelter for displaced families, guiding students through disrupted school terms, coordinating operations with an NGO, redesigning trauma-sensitive community spaces, or simply providing quiet stability in the aftermath—this book was written with you in mind. You may be the first to arrive or the last to leave. You could be trained or self-taught. You might be holding everything together with spreadsheets, prayers, whiteboards, or water bottles. Regardless of your tools, your presence matters.

Across borders and cultures, I have witnessed what happens when leaders prioritize emotional intelligence over authority. When they manage their own stress before reacting to others. When they listen before they take action. When they root communication in dignity and create environments that soothe. When they pause—not to procrastinate—but to lead with clarity. These leaders are the reason communities rebuild—not just physically but also emotionally.

You will not find disaster response protocols or legal frameworks here. This book is not intended to replace operational handbooks; rather, it aims to complement them. Its purpose is to bridge the emotional gap between policy and the individual, supporting you as you support others—especially when the media departs and the most challenging work remains.

You might be a teacher, a midwife, a counselor, a local government worker, a community elder, a youth advocate, a coach, a parent, a faith leader, or a neighbor with sharp instincts. You could be in uniform, wearing sandals, or in borrowed shoes. But if you have ever found yourself providing structure, presence, or peace when everything else was falling apart—then this book is for you.

It will not tell you how to feel—but it will provide you with tools for navigating what arises. It will not give you scripts—but it will offer language when words fail. And it will not promise certainty—but it will help you find clarity in chaos and calm in complexity.

You do not have to be perfect to lead through disaster.

You simply need to be present, prepared, and willing to lead from within.

Introduction

The Storm Is Only the Beginning

Disasters do not end when the water recedes, the wind dies down, or the sirens fade. For those who remain—community leaders, volunteers, teachers, aid workers, healthcare workers, and neighbors—the true storm often begins in the aftermath. The emotional debris is just as real as the physical. It lingers in disrupted routines, unspoken grief, and the overwhelming pressure to hold others together while still trying to breathe.

Before we start, think about this: Where were you the last time everything changed in an instant? And how did you react when others looked to you for calm?

Whether you are in a flood-prone village in the Philippines, leading a shelter following an earthquake in Haiti, rebuilding a school in South India, guiding relief teams in Nigeria, coordinating displacement shelters in Arctic Canada, stabilizing communities after a hurricane in Jamaica, organizing recovery efforts in Uzbekistan, supporting evacuees in California, assisting families in Indonesia after an unexpected landslide, or navigating the cross-border grief after the 2025 India plane crash that claimed over 279 lives and affected both local and UK families—this book was written with you in mind. Across countries and crises, one truth remains: emotional leadership is not optional; it is essential.

Even corporate leaders responsible for team well-being, corporate social responsibility, or global workforce stabilization will find tools to support emotional leadership during times of rapid change.

Whether leading a university department through institutional upheaval, designing global study abroad risk management plans, or guiding international student communities through disruption, these principles apply to both higher education and corporate sectors alike.

Too often, response efforts focus solely on logistics—where to go, what to bring, and how quickly to move. However, in the hours and days following a disaster, people need more than direction. They require steadiness, support, presence, and clarity. They need someone who can bring a small measure of calm into the chaos. That person is often not a specialist or government official. It is the teacher who stays behind, the faith leader who listens, the midwife who adjusts care without electricity, the elder who gathers the displaced beneath temporary shelters, the volunteer who picks up the phone, and the community member who chooses to speak even when their voice trembles.

Emotional presence is not emphasized nearly enough. Yet according to the World Health Organization's Psychological First Aid framework, the first and most effective steps in disaster recovery involve establishing safety, restoring calm, and fostering connection. These steps are not the exclusive domain of experts; they are human abilities—not titles. They are powerful, accessible, and necessary in every language and setting.

Global research continues to affirm what communities have always known: relationships are the backbone of recovery. Studies from the International Federation of Red Cross and Red Crescent Societies show that local leaders—when equipped with communication tools and emotional regulation practices—are often the most trusted and effective anchors during recovery. Similarly, reports from UNICEF emphasize that children process trauma more adaptively when surrounded by calm, grounded adults. What you model, what you say, and how you lead after a crisis leaves a lasting imprint, extending far beyond the event itself.

This book serves as a companion for that journey. It is neither a technical manual nor a policy guide. It provides a practical, culturally adaptable framework for stepping up as a leader when everything seems to be unraveling. It is rooted in emotional intelligence, grounded in real-world application, and designed to support you during some of the most human moments of your life.

Throughout these pages, you will find guidance on emotional regulation under pressure, communicating across cultural boundaries, restoring dignity after disruption, and supporting the emotional recovery of those around you—without losing yourself in the process. Whether you are a shelter coordinator ensuring safety and structure, a principal helping students return to class, a government liaison managing cross-sector partnerships, or a youth leader rebuilding trust in a disrupted community—this book offers insights you can apply in any situation: clarity in communication, steadiness in crisis, and leadership with integrity.

Here, you will not be asked to rise above your reality. Instead, you will be invited to remain present within it—with tools to care for your nervous system, structure your response, support your community, and preserve your energy. Whether you are facing a sudden natural disaster or navigating the long tail of systemic neglect, the guidance in these pages is designed to accompany you across borders, languages, and roles.

Disaster response is never easy. However, it becomes bearable—and even transformative—when those involved are acknowledged, supported, and equipped. You don't need to be perfect. You don't need to know everything. You only need to be willing to care genuinely, lead honestly, and stay emotionally connected to yourself and those around you.

You will soon be introduced to the Global Leadership Framework—a practical guide for navigating disaster leadership with steadiness, emotional integrity, and cultural awareness. This framework will accompany you throughout the book, helping you to lead from within even when conditions remain uncertain.

The storm isn't just about what happened; it's about who you're willing to become in the aftermath. And that journey starts here.

Throughout this book, you will find Global Reality Checks—brief, real-world snapshots from 2025 and beyond. These moments, drawn from both international headlines and overlooked corners of daily life, serve as reminders that leadership under pressure is no longer theoretical. The urgency is now. And the leader is often you.

Author's Note

Why I Wrote This Book

I am not a therapist, a first responder, a licensed clinician, or a government official.

I am someone who has lived through storm after storm—both personally and professionally—and made the choice to lead through them.

This book was not written from the sidelines. It was built from the ground up—shaped by years of catastrophe work both in the field and at the desk. I've served policyholders on the front lines and supported teams behind the scenes—navigating pressure, emotional labor, and the human cost of disaster response. These environments showed me firsthand how recovery doesn't just depend on logistics—it depends on leadership. Real, human leadership.

The *Leading After the Storm* framework emerged from those lived experiences, conversations with overwhelmed professionals, and global research on emotional intelligence and cultural resilience. I've witnessed communities that held together not because of external resources—but because someone, often unseen, chose to stay steady, stay present, and lead with care.

Some stories in this book reflect actual events; others have been adapted to protect privacy and increase cross-cultural relevance. What binds them all is emotional truth. The names may change. The pain and perseverance are universal.

This work is personal. That's why it's published under the *Efficient Adjuster*™ brand. Because true leadership—especially in crisis work—isn't about titles or checklists. It's about presence, communication, and emotional clarity. These are not soft skills. They are survival skills. And they are more essential than ever.

My goal was never to write a clinical manual. My goal was to create something grounded, something usable, something you could return to when the cameras fade but the pressure continues—when what's at stake is not only recovery, but human dignity.

If you see yourself in these pages, thank you.

If you are still walking through the fog, keep going.

And if you ever wonder whether your leadership makes a difference—this is your reminder: it does.

Stay grounded. Stay honest.

And lead from the heart.

— Dr. Karissa Thomas

Founder, Efficient Adjuster™

The Global Leadership Framework: Leading After the Storm

This framework outlines the core leadership rhythm that guides this book. It is designed to serve leaders across diverse cultural, geographic, and institutional contexts—whether coordinating disaster response, guiding a school community, managing a shelter, or stabilizing a village, city, or workplace after upheaval.

Emotional Centering

The Foundation of Leadership Stability

- Regulate your own nervous system before leading others.
- Recognize emotional aftershock as a normal part of leadership.
- Pause and steady yourself before making decisions.

Communication and Trust

The First Bridge to Others

- Speak with clarity, compassion, and cultural awareness.
- Use inclusive language that respects the lived realities of your community.
- Build trust through transparency—not control, speed, or overpromising.

Cultural Coordination

Aligning with Community Realities

- Respect local wisdom, community intelligence, and spiritual rhythms.
- Partner with elders, grassroots organizers, and relational anchors.
- Adapt systems to honor cultural, historical, and relational context.

Long-Term Meaning and Recovery

The Outcome of Emotionally Intelligent Leadership

- Design spaces that foster belonging, dignity, and emotional safety.
- Preserve cultural identity, memory, and spiritual continuity.
- Support meaning-making, collective resilience, and future leadership development.

PART I

Grounding Yourself

Before you can coordinate others, you must learn to steady yourself.

Leadership after a disaster does not begin with strategy—it begins with breath. It begins in the quiet, disorienting moments when your chest tightens, your thoughts race, and the world feels too loud for clarity. These are not signs of weakness; they are signs of impact. And if you've experienced them, you are not alone.

This first section invites you inward—not to retreat, but to reconnect. Before we talk about organizing others, we begin with your internal compass. Here, you will learn how to anchor yourself amid emotional chaos, recognize your own stress signals, and lead from a place of humanity—not just responsibility.

You might find yourself walking into rooms where everyone is waiting for you to speak. You could be guiding others while privately grieving. You may appear calm while your own nervous system is frayed. These chapters serve as a reminder: emotional regulation is not a performance—it is a practice. It is how you lead without losing yourself in the process.

You are not expected to remain unshaken. You are expected to remain present. And presence begins here—with your breath, your body, and your willingness to pause before the next difficult thing begins.

Chapter 1

When the Ground Shakes Inside You

The Hidden Aftershock: Emotional Toll of Disaster Leadership

Disasters do not just destroy buildings. They fracture routines, upend relationships, and displace our sense of safety from within. Long after the winds quiet or the floodwaters recede, the internal storm persists. People look around and ask: What now? What next? Who's going to lead?

> "Disaster doesn't just damage structures. It destabilizes the self."

And sometimes, the answer is you—whether you chose it or not.

That moment—when eyes turn toward you—often lacks applause or affirmation. It can feel isolating. Heavy. Even unfair. You may still be trying to process your own loss when you're asked to bear the weight of others. You might be navigating private grief while being called to provide public strength. This is the invisible cost of disaster leadership: the expectation to function while still hurting, to decide while still disoriented, to show up while still unsure.

And yet, it is in these raw, unguarded moments that real leadership begins—not the kind rooted in title, but in truth. The emotional toll doesn't stem solely from the event itself. It arises from what follows: the long nights without answers, the endless decisions, the compassion fatigue, and the silence that comes when others assume you've "got it handled." When your calm is mistaken for invincibility, and your presence is viewed as a substitute for having all the answers.

But even here, in the midst of emotional aftershock, there is purpose. There is power in acknowledging the toll without being defined by it. Because when you lead while healing, you show others that resilience is not perfection—it is presence. Sometimes, your willingness to remain in the moment—shaken, but still steady—is the very thing that helps others find the courage to stay as well.

Leadership While Wounded: Responding Before You Feel Ready

What happens when you are also shaken? When the weight of it all rests heavily on your shoulders, while your heart still hasn't caught up with what just occurred? This is the hidden cost of leadership in crisis: the assumption that, simply because you are standing, you are ready.

The truth is, most people who step into leadership after a disaster do so with trembling hands. They are not unshaken—they are simply choosing to move while still breaking open. They respond not because they feel powerful, but because silence feels heavier. And often, it is because no one else will.

That courage deserves recognition. But it also requires care.

Trauma Layering and Emotional Disorientation

In the emotional fog following a crisis, disorientation is common. Time stretches, and memory fragments. Emotions surface unexpectedly—grief, guilt, irritability, and helplessness. These are not signs of weakness; they reflect the nervous system's response to threat and overwhelm. In many cultures, these internal shifts go unspoken. Communities may gather to repair what was materially lost, but emotionally, people are expected to carry on quietly, strongly, and without pause.

But unprocessed emotions do not disappear; they redirect. They manifest in miscommunication, short tempers, or exhaustion that no amount of rest can mend. When a leader carries that silently, it seeps into the entire team or community.

> "You can't lead others to safety if your inner world is still on fire."

Biology of Overwhelm: It's Not Just You

You are not exempt from the emotional toll simply because others look to you for guidance. In fact, your nervous system is likely absorbing more than you realize. The pressure to appear composed, calm others, and make the right decisions—these expectations compound what psychologists refer to as layered trauma.

Dr. Bessel van der Kolk, trauma expert and author of "The Body Keeps the Score," explains that traumatic stress disrupts the brain's ability to process time, choice, and clarity. Your body may remain reactive long after the danger has passed. Your voice may tremble—even when your mind insists you keep pushing.

These experiences are not limitations; they are signals. Listening to them—without judgment—can help you become a more grounded and trustworthy leader.

Case in Point: Kerala Floods, 2018

During the 2018 floods in Kerala, India, many school teachers and local officials became de facto leaders in shelters, despite having lost their homes and loved ones. They were still grieving—but they organized food lines, reassured frightened children, and helped elderly evacuees feel noticed. Their leadership was not born from certainty but from courage amid personal loss.

Internal Awareness Is Crisis Preparedness

You do not need to wait until you are fully healed to show up. But you do need to check in with yourself honestly:

- Are you making decisions out of panic or out of clarity?
- Are you addressing genuine needs—or reacting to pressure?
- Are you taking on too much without any space to breathe?

These are not indulgent questions. They are intelligent ones. They prevent collapse. They sustain your ability to serve.

The Flood at Camp Mystic
Texas Hill Country | Early July 2025

In early July 2025, torrential rainstorms swept across Central Texas, triggering flash floods that devastated parts of Kerr County. In just two hours, the Guadalupe River rose more than six and a half meters, fueled by over 25 centimeters of overnight rainfall. It reached its second-highest recorded level before the river gauge was overwhelmed and stopped transmitting data.

One of the hardest-hit areas was Camp Mystic, a Christian summer camp along the Guadalupe River. With over 700 campers on site—many between seven and seventeen years old—the situation quickly turned into a full-scale emergency as floodwaters rose, cabins were flooded, and communication lines failed. But the destruction extended beyond the campgrounds. Families, residents, and entire neighborhoods across Kerr County were also caught in the storm's path, many experiencing sudden evacuations and devastating losses. In the aftermath, dozens of lives were lost across Texas, including many children. Among the missing were campers and at least one counselor from

> "What looks like confusion may be the nervous system trying to survive."

6

Camp Mystic, casting a long shadow of grief over families, communities, and everyone who witnessed the tragedy.

Survivors described harrowing scenes—clinging to trees, rooftops, and floating debris. Parents flooded emergency lines and social media with pleas. Emergency teams worked around the clock using helicopters, rescue boats, drones, and ground search units. It was a moment of shared heartbreak—and a test of every leadership system in place.

But this story is not just about what was lost. It is about what must be built.

It is a call to prepare before the storm, not react after. To design systems that hold under pressure. To coordinate across agencies, not in competition but in compassion. To practice emotional regulation, clear communication, and trauma-informed decision-making—especially when the timeline is short and the pressure is high.

Because this is not just a leadership issue. It is a human one.

Disaster does not ask whether we are ready. It simply arrives.

And when it does, we will not rise to the moment—we will fall to the level of our preparation.

That preparation is emotional. Structural. Cultural. Communal.

And it belongs to all of us.

So what is the solution?

We build leadership systems rooted in care, not control.

We create emergency plans that account for trauma, not just timelines.

We train teams to regulate, communicate, and coordinate—under pressure.

And we lead not only with protocols, but with presence.

This is why we lead.

To be the calm in the flood.

The voice in the silence.

The system that does not collapse when others do.

And the human presence that makes recovery possible.

Emotional Integrity as a Leadership Anchor

Emotional integrity in leadership starts not with external control, but with internal awareness. By naming your feelings, you enable others to do the same. By modeling presence, you remind people they are not alone. And by leading with humanity, you restore dignity where it has been taken away.

Emotional integrity is not about being emotionally raw in every moment; it is about being emotionally real. In disaster contexts, where grief fills the air and fear lurks just beneath the surface, people crave authenticity more than certainty. They do not need a leader who pretends to be unaffected; they need one who can acknowledge the weight of the moment while still guiding the way forward. That kind of emotional honesty fosters safety. It says: You are not alone in feeling overwhelmed. And together, we can still take the next step.

This is especially vital when leading teams who are also experiencing the disaster themselves. By giving language to the invisible—stress, numbness, sadness, fatigue—you create a culture where emotional reactions are normalized rather than suppressed. In that space, people are more likely to stay engaged, communicate clearly, and support one another. Emotional integrity creates a ripple effect: it invites others to bring their full selves to the work, fostering a leadership environment rooted not in performance, but in presence. That's where trust lives. That's where recovery begins.

Field Reflection: Eastern Cape, South Africa

In a rural village in the Eastern Cape of South Africa, a young woman began coordinating clean water deliveries even as her own family farm struggled due to drought. She cried privately each night but showed up every morning to organize her neighbors. Eventually, others joined her—not because she was the loudest, but because she was dependable. Her self-awareness became a quiet invitation to collective leadership.

2020 Snapshot:
Coordinating Calm Amid Crisis
(United Arab Emirates, Pandemic Response)

During the global pandemic of 2020–2021, the United Arab Emirates faced the challenge of protecting its diverse population across cities, industries, and communities. With over 200 nationalities living and working within its borders, leaders were tasked with not only delivering rapid medical care but also managing clear, culturally sensitive communication across languages and sectors.

Government health authorities collaborated with private sector companies, community organizations, and international partners to coordinate large-scale testing, quarantine protocols, and vaccination campaigns. Public messaging was translated into multiple languages to ensure clarity for all residents, while hotels, convention centers, and converted facilities provided safe isolation housing during high-risk periods.

Throughout the response, emotional steadiness and logistical clarity became critical leadership traits—balancing public safety with economic stability while maintaining calm across a global workforce far from home. The UAE's response gained international recognition for its speed, coordination, and ability to maintain both order and reassurance in the face of unprecedented uncertainty.

Closing Insight: Lead Yourself First

This chapter is not an invitation to dwell on emotion. It is a call to respect it. Only when we acknowledge the weight we carry can we begin to lead without collapsing under it.

Disasters shake the ground beneath us. Yet, it is the unseen fault lines—the emotional ones—that determine how we rise.

And how we help others rise with us.

Too often, leaders are celebrated for their output and endurance, yet they are rarely supported in the quiet work of self-stabilization. However, that inner work is not indulgent; it is essential. Ignoring your own emotional landscape does not make you stronger; it makes you brittle. Brittle leaders break under prolonged pressure. Respecting your internal signals—grief, fear, fatigue, compassion—is not weakness; it's wisdom. It's the leadership behind the leadership.

When we pause to acknowledge our emotional burden, we allow ourselves to act with integrity instead of reactivity. We transition from merely surviving the moment to intentionally shaping it. That presence becomes our most powerful gift—not only for ourselves but also for those who look to us when the world feels too heavy to bear. The truth is, others will take their cues from how we lead ourselves first.

And in doing so, we don't just weather the storm—we become the reason others believe they can, too.

▶ *Related Toolkit: 5-Minute Reset Routines (Appendix B)*

Daily Anchor for Leading Anyway

As I step forward from this chapter, I recognize that leadership often begins in the quiet tremors inside my own soul. The world may shift, but I do not have to collapse with it. My steadiness is not the absence of fear, but the choice to remain rooted even as everything moves around me. Each moment of uncertainty becomes an opportunity to strengthen the ground beneath my own feet.

Quietly or aloud, say after me:
"Even when the ground shakes, I stand. My stability is not dependent on my circumstances. I am steady. I am grounded."

🌎 CHAPTER 1 LEADERSHIP SNAPSHOT 🌎

FRAMEWORK IN ACTION

This chapter supports two key components of the *Global Leadership Framework*:

Emotional Centering: By inviting leaders to pause, regulate, and reconnect with their own nervous systems before making decisions or guiding others.

Long-Term Meaning and Recovery: By addressing the invisible emotional costs of leadership and normalizing the personal impact of leading through crisis.

KEY LEADERSHIP TAKEAWAYS

- Emotional aftershock is a normal leadership response—not a weakness.
- Presence matters more than perfection.
- Leadership often begins before you feel ready.
- Self-regulation creates safety for others.
- Integrity means acknowledging the weight you carry, not pretending it isn't there.

REFLECTIVE JOURNAL QUESTIONS

1 What emotional or physical signals indicate that I'm nearing overwhelm?

2 How can I maintain emotional integrity when I feel unsteady?

3 Where do I feel pressured to be "the strong one," and how can I allow space for my own humanity?

CULTURAL INSIGHT

In many Indigenous and collectivist cultures, leadership is based on attentiveness and calm—not control. Leadership can manifest in silent watchfulness, ritual, or shared decision-making, rather than solely in verbal direction. This chapter honors those traditions by affirming that leadership through presence is valid, powerful, and often lifesaving.

USE THIS SECTION TO:

▶ Begin leadership team debriefs or self-awareness workshops
▶ Train volunteer leaders on the emotional cost of service
▶ Reinforce the human side of disaster coordination
▶ Support team members who are emotionally impacted but still leading

Chapter 2

The Power of Calm Leadership

The Leadership Power of Presence

In the midst of chaos, it is not always the loudest voice or the most brilliant plan that leads; rather, it is the most grounded presence. Across continents, cultures, and crises, people instinctively look for safety—not just in strategy, but in individuals. That sense of safety is conveyed not only through words but also through tone, posture, rhythm, and stillness. Whether in a crowded shelter in the Philippines, a rural clinic in Kenya, a school gymnasium in the United States, or a city square in Brazil, people often determine whether to trust you based on how composed you appear in the moment.

"Calm is not a mood. It is a leadership skill."

That is why calm is more than a leadership quality—it is a survival tool. And it is contagious.

Presence is what people cling to when everything else feels unstable. It is not about charisma, eloquence, or formal titles—it is about embodiment. When you are anchored in yourself, others can anchor to you. In disaster zones, refugee camps, urban recovery efforts, or informal community gatherings, the human nervous system responds in the same way: it scans for cues—Are we safe? Can this person be trusted? Is someone grounded—not in control of the world, but in control of themselves? If your presence communicates regulation, steadiness, and care, it transcends language and signals stability before a single instruction is given.

This is why calm leadership cannot be faked. People across cultures can sense the difference between performative composure and genuine groundedness. If your breath is shallow, your body tense, or your voice strained, those around you will feel the dissonance, even if they do not speak your language. However, when your calm is rooted in truth—even if imperfect—it fosters connection. In that safety, people begin to organize, settle, and trust again. Whether you are leading through wildfire, displacement, political unrest, or community grief, your presence is not just part of the leadership equation; it is the equation. Calm does not just lead; it stabilizes, heals, and gives others permission to do the same.

Inner Coherence Over Outward Performance

In disaster-impacted communities worldwide, calm manifests in various forms. In some places, it appears as quiet determination; in others, it takes the shape of measured speech or purposeful stillness. What matters most is not outward performance but internal coherence. People instinctively know when a leader is centered—and when that calm is merely a façade. Pretending often heightens fear, while genuine presence—a combination of steadiness and sincerity—builds trust even in the most unstable circumstances.

Grounding Through Breath and Body Awareness

Regulating your nervous system during a disaster does not mean being unaffected. It means staying connected to your body, your breath, and your ability to pause—even when everything around you demands urgency.

It starts with breathing. Not exaggerated or theatrical, but slow, intentional breaths that signal safety to your nervous system. Research in polyvagal theory confirms that specific patterns—such as inhaling for four counts, holding for two, and exhaling for six—can help shift the body from a stress response into a more grounded state. This practice will not eliminate the crisis, but it will allow you to face it with greater clarity and presence.

Grounding is helpful as well. It can be as simple as pressing your feet firmly into the floor, clasping your hands, or feeling the weight of your shoulders. These subtle acts are often dismissed as trivial—but in high-stress environments, the nervous system looks for anchors. Grounding sends a message: I am here. I am still connected.

Voice and Rhythm as Tools for Stability

Your tone of voice is just as important. When you speak rapidly, your nervous system is likely operating faster than your mind can fully process. Slowing your speech creates a rhythm that others can connect with. Humans are wired to mirror the emotional states around them. That is why panic spreads quickly—but so does calm.

You won't feel calm all the time. That's normal. That's human. What matters is not avoiding overwhelm but having the tools to return to your center when it counts. You don't have to maintain perfect regulation at every moment—but you must learn how to recover it.

Case Example
Earthquake Recovery in Puerto Rico

After a series of tremors in southern Puerto Rico, a school administrator began each day by gathering her staff in a moment of silence followed by a shared breath. Her calm presence became an emotional anchor. Staff and students reported feeling safer simply because her tranquility was visible, consistent, and sincere. Even without ideal resources, her regulation shaped the tone of the entire shelter-school environment.

Regulation, Not Suppression

In many cultures, particularly those with generational trauma or histories of systemic instability, leaders are expected to suppress emotions, appearing stoic and composed at any cost. However, emotional regulation is not the same as suppression. Suppression conceals what is real, whereas regulation engages with it. Suppression can harden you, while regulation offers flexibility—enough to bend without breaking.

Suppression may seem like strength in the short term, but over time, it corrodes connection—both to oneself and to others. When leaders suppress, they often become distant, rigid, and emotionally unavailable, creating environments where others feel unsafe expressing vulnerability. The unintended consequence is a culture of silence— where pain is minimized, support is withheld, and trust slowly erodes. This doesn't just affect morale; it undermines the very cohesion needed for recovery.

Regulation, by contrast, invites a different kind of leadership— one rooted in emotional awareness, not avoidance. It involves acknowledging the wave without being swept away by it. It means breathing through the fear rather than suppressing it. It means recognizing when your body is in overdrive and consciously choosing to return to your center. In a crisis, people don't need you to be invulnerable. They need to know that calm is attainable. That it's okay to feel. That it's safe to exhale. Regulation provides that safety—first to the leader, and then to everyone observing them navigate the storm.

Presence Over Perfection

The people you serve do not need perfection; they need presence. They need someone who can remain in the moment, even when it becomes shaky. Someone who can breathe when they cannot. Someone who chooses to model steadiness—not because the crisis is small, but because abandoning self-awareness during these moments is simply too costly.

Perfection is often a mask—a performance rooted in fear of getting it wrong. However, in disaster leadership, perfection creates distance. It can make you seem unreach-able, untouchable, or out of sync with the very people you're trying to serve. Presence, on the other hand, does the opposite. It invites closeness. It reminds others that leadership is not about being above the moment, but rather within it—fully engaged, emotionally honest, and available in real time.

> "In crisis, your nervous system communicates before your mouth does."

When you choose presence over performance, you create space for others to be human too. You give permission for grief to surface, for questions to be asked, and for help to be offered and received. You transform leadership from a pedestal into a practice—one that says, "I may not have all the answers, but I'm not leaving. I'm right here with you." In the aftermath of a crisis, that kind of presence becomes a life-line. Not because it fixes everything—but because it reminds people that they don't have to face everything alone.

Conflicting Commands in the Middle of the Storm

The storm continued to rage as city officials gathered in the emergency operations center. Monitors lining the walls displayed real-time updates—flooded roads, rising river levels, and scattered power outages. The air in the room was thick with urgency, yet beneath the tension lay something more perilous: confusion.

Department heads gathered at separate tables, speaking into radios and issuing commands to their teams on the ground. One department ordered barricades to be set up along Main Street. Another depart-ment, unaware of the first order, redirected ambulances along the same route to avoid blocked highways. Emergency management attempted to coordinate efforts, but messages began to overlap. Resources were deployed in opposite directions. The public information offi-cer awaited final guidance before releasing statements to the public, but there was none to give. No one wanted to override anyone else's authority. The fear of overstepping or undermining a colleague created a silent hesitation.

Outside, responders were waiting for clarity that was not coming.

It was not that these leaders were incapable; each was skilled in their respective fields. The issue lay in the absence of a unified voice amid an evolving storm. In moments of crisis, conflicting orders can inflict as much damage as delayed action. When coordination falters, lives linger in that gap.

Finally, one leader stood up—not shouting or blaming. Calmly yet firmly, she called the room to attention. She reviewed the competing orders, highlighted the contradictions, and redirected the team toward a unified plan. She did not demand control; she provided clarity.

Leadership in disaster often requires exactly this: not louder voices, but clearer ones.

2025 Snapshot: Leadership Amid Canada's Wildfires

In the summer of 2025, wildfires devastated Canada's forests at an unprecedented pace. Entire towns faced evacuation within hours. The smoke darkened skies not only over Canada but also drifted across borders into parts of the United States. As flames spread, it was often local leaders—tribal councils, small-town mayors, fire chiefs, and volunteer coordinators—who emerged as the first steady voices amid the chaos. They balanced evacuations while their own families packed to leave, spoke calmly to frightened residents, and organized resources even as air quality reached hazardous levels. When national systems became overwhelmed, these local leaders stood between fear and order—managing not just logistics, but emotional survival.

Closing Insight: You Are the Anchor

This work is not easy, but it is essential. You may not be able to control what is happening around you, but you can learn to calm what is occurring within you. From that place—your breath, your voice, your grounded energy—you offer something that transcends language and logistics: the felt experience of safety. That gift alone can provide people with enough hope and steadiness to keep going.

> "Emotional regulation isn't about ignoring fear— it's about not transferring it."

When everything around you feels unstable, your grounded presence becomes more than leadership—it becomes oxygen. People may not remember every word you said, but they will remember how your energy made them feel. In a world where panic is contagious, so is calm. Your ability to stay centered—through breath, body, and voice—creates a ripple effect that helps others regulate, make decisions, and move forward.

You will not always feel ready. You may question your strength. But anchoring yourself does not require perfection; it requires practice. Each time you pause before reacting, each time you breathe instead of bracing, you reinforce a new kind of power—quiet, steady, and transformative. And even if no one applauds it, that invisible offering of emotional steadiness may be the very thing that holds a family together, settles a team, or makes one more hour of recovery possible.

You are not the storm. You are the anchor. And that is more than enough.

▶ *Related Toolkit: 5-Minute Reset Routines (Appendix B)*

Daily Anchor for Leading Anyway

I release the need to react. I allow calm to rise inside me, even when others are overcome by emotion or urgency. My calm leadership is not passive — it is my power. I create space for clarity to emerge, for thoughtful decisions to unfold, and for others to find steadiness in my presence. This is the leadership I choose to embody.

> *Quietly or aloud, say after me:*
> **"I lead with calm. My presence sets the tone. My peace makes room for solutions."**

🌐 CHAPTER 2 LEADERSHIP SNAPSHOT 🌐

FRAMEWORK IN ACTION

This chapter strengthens two foundational pillars of the *Global Leadership Framework*:

Emotional Centering: By equipping leaders with tangible practices for nervous system regulation and steady presence.

Communication and Trust: By reinforcing how tone, breath, and emotional regulation establish credibility and calm in high-stress environments.

KEY LEADERSHIP TAKEAWAYS

- ▶ Calm is not passive—it is a strategic leadership tool.
- ▶ Regulation is more effective than emotional suppression.
- ▶ People respond to your tone and presence before your words.
- ▶ Inner coherence creates outer stability for teams and communities.
- ▶ Leadership is not about flawless performance—it's about emotional availability.

REFLECTIVE JOURNAL QUESTIONS

1. When I am under pressure, how does my nervous system respond—and how can I bring myself back to center?

2. Do I confuse suppression with strength? How can I demonstrate authentic regulation instead?

3. What daily practices can I use to maintain calm without emotionally shutting down?

CULTURAL INSIGHT

Across various cultures—including Indigenous, African, and Eastern traditions—leadership is frequently expressed through rhythm, presence, and stillness. In these contexts, a calm leader embodies wisdom. Chapter 2 supports this idea by highlighting regulation, breath, and composure as universal languages of safety and strength.

USE THIS SECTION TO:

- Train crisis leaders, school staff, or NGO workers in high-stress response roles
- Support staff retreats, resilience workshops, or trauma-informed leadership circles
- Encourage frontline professionals to lead from grounded presence
- Help leaders model emotional stability in culturally diverse teams

Chapter 3

Leading in the Fog

GLOBAL REALITY CHECK
CRISIS AT YOUR DOORSTEP

You can no longer afford to look away.

Crisis doesn't just happen somewhere else. It appears in grocery aisles, on highways, in airports, classrooms, and malls. It can strike quietly or violently—but always without warning. When it does, someone must step up. Not perfect, but present.

On June 26, 2025, north Houston came to a halt. A 64-year-old woman in a folding chair blocked both lanes of I-45 after crashing into an 18-wheeler and brandishing a firearm. She sat there for five hours. Alone. Armed. Surrounded by SWAT. Commuters were frozen in place. Tension filled the air like an unbroken storm.

Just days earlier, on June 22, 2025, inside Houston's Galleria Mall, a suspected shoplifter sprinted past families and jumped over the second-floor railing—crashing onto the ice rink below. His legs shattered. Panic spread

> "Uncertainty does not disqualify you from leadership. It invites you to lead differently."

quickly. What started as a normal shopping trip turned into a crisis—immediately.

That same week, on June 20, 2025, in San Antonio, a suspected car break-in escalated into a six-hour SWAT standoff. Nearby homes were evacuated. Streets were locked down. Families watched from their windows, unsure of what might happen next.

And on June 24, 2025, at Palma de Mallorca Airport in Spain, part of the ceiling inside the arrivals hall collapsed—glass and debris falling onto baggage belts and passengers. No lives were lost. But the message was clear: even the places we trust most can fail without warning—and the calm of those nearby can influence what happens next.

These are more than stories; they serve as signals. The pace of disruption is speeding up. Crisis is no longer limited to distant disasters. It's becoming part of everyday life—in cities and towns, terminals and neighborhoods, homes and institutions.

This is the era we live in now.

Not everyone will be trained to respond.
Not everyone will have clear instructions.
But someone will need to step forward.

That someone might be you.

Leadership today is not about titles.
It is about awareness—finding it in moments others overlook.
Grounded presence—staying calm when panic spreads.
Compassionate clarity—speaking up when silence takes hold.
Preparedness is not fear.
It is *attentiveness*.
It is recognizing when something is off—before it unravels.
It is noticing the shifts in energy, behavior, movement, and voice.

A hesitation.
A sudden quiet.
A raised voice.
A missed step.
A subtle change that means something deeper is stirring.

The next storm may not be loud.
It may begin with a glance.
A delay.
A breath held too long.
A ceiling cracking above your head.

You do not need to be perfect.
You need to be present.
You need to be prepared.
You need to be steady—before the world tips sideways.

Framework in Action

The Global Leadership Framework emphasizes that in moments of disorientation—whether in a shopping mall, freeway, or airport—leadership begins with emotional presence. In the incidents across Texas and Spain, what shifted outcomes was not the presence of a manual, but the presence of people who stayed calm, observed the unfolding environment, and made micro-decisions that prevented further harm. This is *leadership in the fog*—moving without full clarity, but grounded in awareness, emotional steadiness, and relational attunement.

When systems lag and instructions falter, what remains is *you*. Your tone, your posture, your first response. In moments like these, preparedness is less about having the right gear and more about having the right internal compass.

> "When the map disappears, your clarity becomes the compass."

Reflective Journal Prompt

Think of a time when something around you felt "off" before it escalated.

How did you respond? What signals do you now recognize in hindsight that could guide your presence in future uncertain moments?

Collective Model Highlight

In many Indigenous North American traditions, *watchers* or *scouts* were respected roles within a tribe—people trained not only to look outward for physical danger but to sense subtle shifts in emotional or environmental energy. These quiet leaders were often the first to notice disturbances—well before others detected anything wrong. Their presence was not rooted in power, but in perception. Today's fog requires that same kind of leadership.

* • • ○ • • •

Making Decisions Without Certainty

Disaster strips away the illusion of time. Choices that would normally unfold over days must be made in minutes. People turn to you with questions you cannot fully answer. They look to you for direction while your own mind grapples with uncertainty. Yet leadership does not wait for clarity. It demands presence—especially when the fog is dense and nothing feels certain.

In those moments, the weight of leadership is not merely logistical—it is profoundly emotional. Every decision feels magnified, shrouded by uncertainty. You may fear being wrong. You may worry that one misstep could unravel fragile trust or endanger lives. Yet, waiting too long can bring its own consequences. The people around you aren't always asking for perfection—they're asking for movement. For someone to speak into the silence, to break the paralysis, to offer a next step, even if that step is small.

Leading through uncertainty means learning to act with humility, not haste. It requires admitting what you don't know while still offering what you can: presence, logic, care, and a steady voice. It involves making the best possible choice with the information available—and then adjusting as the situation evolves. The fog won't always lift before you move, but your willingness to lead with courage and integrity through the fog becomes a beacon for others trying to find their way.

The Responsibility of Every Decision

This is where many leaders hesitate. Not because they are unqualified, but because they comprehend the weight of responsibility and consequences that accompany each decision. After a crisis, even the smallest choice feels monumental. Where should families go? What information should be shared? Who receives aid first? Each answer carries implications. And when the stakes involve human lives, the fear of making a wrong choice can be paralyzing.

However understandable, paralysis does not equate to leadership. When communities are engaged and danger approaches, hesitation can swiftly result in harm. That is why decision-making under pressure is not merely a gift of the elite—it is a learnable, repeatable practice rooted in emotional regulation and mindfulness.

Understanding the Brain Under Threat

The human brain, when under threat, narrows its focus. Neurologically, fear shifts us into survival mode. Cognitive resources are redirected away from long-term reasoning and toward immediate action. Accessing reflection, empathy, and strategy becomes more difficult. This is not a failure; it is biology.

But it also means that trauma-informed leadership begins with a single act: pausing. Even brief moments of breath, orientation, or internal grounding can restore access to your clearest thinking. This is not indulgent; it is essential. Reactivity fuels chaos, while regulation restores leadership.

This biological response is universal—whether you are leading a disaster shelter in Haiti, navigating civil unrest in Sudan, or coordinating emergency teams in New Zealand. When people are afraid, their ability to process complex instructions, empathize with others, or make thoughtful decisions diminishes. Leaders are not exempt from this pattern. In fact, those responsible for others often bear a compounded cognitive load—balancing their own stress while absorbing the group's fear.

Understanding this neurological shift enables leaders to respond with greater compassion and intention. When you observe someone shutting down, escalating, or disengaging, it may not be defiance—it may be the brain protecting itself. Similarly, when you feel foggy, impatient, or scattered, it does not imply you are unfit to lead. Instead, it indicates that your nervous system is working hard to keep you alive.

This is why simple acts—slowing your breath, naming what is happening, drinking water, or taking a moment to step outside—are not luxuries in crisis leadership. They are resets. They reopen the neural pathways needed for empathy, discernment, and complex decision-making. A trauma-informed leader learns not to power through, but to pause—using awareness, not adrenaline, as the fuel for wise action. In doing so, you lead not from reaction, but from regulation—and that shift changes everything.

Predictability Over Perfection

Sometimes, there may not be an ideal path forward. All choices carry risk. Conflicting voices will present differing priorities. In those moments, perfection holds less value than predictability. When people cannot foresee the world, they need to be able to foresee you. If your leadership is rooted in calm, care, and consistency—even in uncertain times—people will follow.

Predictability offers a sense of safety when the world no longer makes sense. It doesn't refer to rigid routines or inflexible plans—it signifies that people can rely on your tone, your timing, your presence. Even if you don't have all the answers, they know when you'll check in. Even if the news isn't good, they trust you to be honest. In a sea of unknowns, your consistency becomes the shoreline by which others orient themselves.

Perfection often creates distance, but predictability builds relationships. It allows teams to breathe, families to adjust, and communities to lean in—even when they're grieving or afraid. When your leadership is steady in rhythm and grounded in care, it sends a quiet but powerful message: I may not control what's coming, but I will show up for it—fully, reliably, and without wavering. Sometimes, that steadiness is the very thing that keeps people from falling apart.

Discernment: Hearing Beyond the Noise

One of the most overlooked leadership skills during a crisis is discernment: the ability to distinguish between what is urgent and what is merely loud. Not every emergency announces itself. Not every outcry demands an immediate response. The best leaders know how to listen deeply—to their own instincts, to the environment, and to the human needs beneath the noise.

This clarity is not tied to authority. It is tied to intention. It comes from knowing your role, honoring your values, and moving from purpose—not pressure.

In the chaos of crisis, volume can be mistaken for importance. Emotions run high, demands come from all directions, and the pressure to respond quickly can cloud your judgment. But discernment calls you to pause, to observe the full picture, and to resist reacting to the loudest voice in the room. It encourages you to notice what's missing, not just

"You don't need perfect answers to lead—you need the courage to decide anyway."

what's visible—to ask, Whose voice isn't being heard? What pain is going unnoticed? What quiet warning signs are we dismissing because something else is grabbing our attention?

True discernment isn't flashy. It's slow, grounded, and requires humility to admit that the obvious answer might not be the right one—and courage to choose a quieter path when the crowd expects spectacle. When leaders practice discernment, they prevent unnecessary harm, preserve energy for what truly matters, and make space for wisdom to guide their actions. It's not just about being reactive; it's about being responsible with what you choose to respond to. In a world overwhelmed by noise, discernment is one of the greatest gifts you can offer.

Case Example
Flood Response in the UK

During the 2014 floods in Somerset, England, local farmers coordinated boat rescues and supply runs before government resources arrived. One farmer, untrained in disaster response, became the point of coordination for multiple villages simply because he acted swiftly, communicated clearly, and remained emotionally steady. His clarity under pressure fostered trust throughout the region.

Case Example
Earthquake Recovery in Chile

In the aftermath of Chile's massive 2010 earthquake, small neighborhood groups known as juntas de vecinos quickly mobilized in cities like Concepción and Talcahuano. Without waiting for formal instructions, these local organizations coordinated food distribution, checked on isolated elderly residents, and established neighborhood watch rotations to prevent looting. Their pre-existing community networks enabled them to respond swiftly and cohesively while larger governmental systems were still assessing the damage. It was their trust in one another—not formal titles—that stabilized the fragile early days following the quake.

When Hierarchy Slows Down Response

In regions where strict hierarchy prevails, many emerging leaders hesitate to act without formal approval. However, disaster does not wait for protocol; it responds to movement. In community after community, the most impactful leaders are rarely those with the highest rank. Instead, they are the individuals who step in when others hesitate, who choose thoughtful action when others are paralyzed, and who lean into service when certainty disappears.

In some cultural contexts, leadership is closely linked to age, gender, status, or institutional authority. Deference is ingrained—young people wait for elders, women wait for men, and civilians wait for officials. However, in the immediate aftermath of a disaster, waiting can cost lives. Roads collapse, communications fail, and decision-makers may be unreachable. In those critical hours, leadership must become fluid. The question is no longer, who has the title? But rather, who sees the need and is willing to respond?

This shift does not reject structure; it recognizes urgency. Some of the most effective disaster responses have come from local farmers organizing evacuation routes, students coordinating aid drop-offs, or shopkeepers transforming storefronts into supply hubs. These leaders do not wait for permission—they respond with presence. They understand that in a crisis, initiative is not rebellion; it is responsibility.

True leadership honors hierarchy *without* being bound by it. It respects the systems in place *while* remaining nimble enough to fill the gaps those systems cannot reach in time. When leadership is viewed not as a possession but as a shared responsibility, communities become more resilient. And in the wake of disaster, that resilience often makes the difference between delay and survival.

Case Example
Flash Flood in Kerala

In India, a school principal organized the evacuation of hundreds of children and families during a sudden flash flood—not because she was instructed to, but because she recognized the danger and acted before bureaucracy could respond. The rain had been relentless for days, but no official evacuation orders had been issued. As water levels surged near the school grounds, she quickly assessed the risk, gathered her staff, and initiated a structured exit plan—moving children to higher ground and coordinating with parents as panic spread through the community.

Using school buses, sidewalks, and even local boats provided by the villagers, she established a temporary safety corridor. Her swift actions, rooted in instinct, care, and a deep understanding of her community, ensured that families were relocated to safer areas before emergency responders arrived. Long after the waters receded, many credited her bravery and calm presence with preventing what could have become a devastating loss of life.

Case Example
Wildfire Response in Australia

In New South Wales, during a series of fast-moving bushfires, a retired nurse emerged as an unlikely leader in her neighborhood when blocked roads and shifting wind patterns delayed fire crews. Lacking formal authority or emergency training, she swiftly assessed her community's immediate needs. Recognizing vulnerable residents who required medication, oxygen, or mobility assistance, she began organizing neighbors into small teams.

Using text chains, handwritten notes, and checklists, she coordinated evacuation routes, monitored medical supplies, and ensured that those unable to drive were transported safely. As the fires approached, her calm, decisive, and inclusive leadership helped stabilize the neighborhood during those critical early hours. Her ability to balance swift action with emotional steadiness prevented panic from taking hold, allowing her community to mobilize effectively while waiting for professional responders. In the aftermath, many residents credited her with saving lives and establishing a sense of order when official systems had yet to arrive.

Case Example
Urban Crisis Response in Shanghai, China

During the resurgence of the pandemic in 2022, parts of Shanghai experienced sudden city-wide lockdowns that disrupted daily life for millions of residents. Apartment complexes transformed into temporary quarantine zones. Due to insufficient city-level staffing, local building managers and volunteer resident coordinators stepped into leadership roles. They organized food deliveries, coordinated medical access for vulnerable residents, and provided emotional support for neighbors isolated for weeks. These informal leaders helped ease tensions, communicated calmly across hundreds of apartments, and established micro-systems of care within large-scale, high-rise isolation zones. In complex urban crises, even small groups of leaders can stabilize entire buildings facing immense social strain.

Crisis Leadership Requires
Courage and Timely Action

Across cultural contexts, stories like these are not exceptions. They serve as reminders that leadership is less about titles and more about courage. In moments of high stakes, the question is not: Do I have the power? The question is: What can I do right now that reflects care, clarity, and responsibility?

You may not always feel ready. You may not always have control. However, you can choose to respond with grounded awareness instead of fear. Respond from discernment, not distraction. Engage from a center that stays steady even when the world around you shifts.

Crisis leadership isn't about waiting for the perfect moment; it's about acting with integrity in the moment at hand. Around the world, we see time and again that those who step forward aren't always the ones with credentials or formal titles. Instead, they often are individuals shaped by hardship, anchored by purpose, and perceptive enough to recognize when hesitation could cost too much.

The courage required is not reckless bravery; it is thoughtful, grounded action. It is the courage to say, "This matters. We cannot wait." Whether you are a village elder in Malawi, a teacher in Beirut, a nurse in New Orleans, or a youth volunteer in Manila, your influence begins when you act from intention, not impulse.

Timely action does not mean rushing; it is responding in alignment with what the moment requires. Sometimes, that involves leading an evacuation; other times, it means sitting with someone in shock and offering a calm voice when the world feels unbearable. It entails knowing when to speak, when to delegate, and when to pause. This type of leadership cannot always be taught in classrooms, but it can be practiced in every crisis, refined through each moment that demands more than fear, and strengthened each time you choose to show up anyway.

The Confidence Framework: Steady When You're Not Sure

The storm had passed, but the damage remained. Roads were flooded. Power was out. Families gathered at a temporary shelter—an elementary school transformed overnight into a place of refuge. Uncertainty hung heavy in the air. Supplies were on the way, but delays were mounting. The teams on site were doing their best, but many lacked formal training. People needed leadership—but clear answers were still hours away.

Maya stood near the front doors. She wasn't a disaster expert or an appointed official. She was a school administrator who had volunteered to open the building when no one else had arrived yet. And now, dozens of eyes were looking to her.

The questions came quickly, echoing concerns that arise in every region when crisis displaces clarity:

"When will help arrive?"

"Is the water safe to drink?"

"Will we sleep here tonight?"

"Who's in charge?"

Maya didn't have all the answers. However, she did possess something else: a framework for remaining steady in the unknown. It lived inside her—not as a script, but as a posture. She went through five simple actions that helped her project calm and restore a sense of order:

1. **Acknowledge what is true.**
   "We are still waiting on confirmation. The delivery team is on the way, but roads are slowing them down."

2. **Name the next immediate step.**
   "In the next hour, we'll do a headcount to ensure everyone is accounted for, especially elders and young children."

3. **Establish a short timeline for re-evaluation.**
   "After that, we'll check in again in two hours with any new updates."

4. **Project steadiness through tone, not volume.**
   Her voice remained measured, unrushed. She slowed her breathing before speaking, signaling calm with her rhythm.

5. **Invite participation, not helpless waiting.**
   "I'll need three volunteers to check in with families needing medical assistance."

Maya's confidence did not come from certainty. It came from grounding herself, regulating her emotions, and offering others something concrete to hold onto. Her approach wasn't magic—it was human. And it worked.

In emergency settings around the world—from hurricane shelters in the Caribbean to flood zones in South Asia to refugee camps in the Middle East—this kind of presence has become a lifeline. The most trusted leaders are often not those with the most knowledge but those who provide the clearest guidance in action.

Confidence under pressure is not a personality trait; it is a practice.

Clarity, next steps, timing, tone, and inclusion—these five elements create a rhythm that others can follow, even when outcomes remain uncertain. You do not have to know everything to lead well. You simply need to offer enough structure in the moment for others to breathe, settle, and move forward with you.

Closing Insight: Steering Through Uncertainty

This is what it means to lead in the fog: not having all the answers but becoming a source of direction when others are lost. It is about acting with integrity, even when the map is unclear, and in doing so, reminding others that even in uncertainty, someone is still steering.

Leadership in uncertainty is not about pretending to see what others cannot; it is about holding the compass steady when the path ahead disappears. In those moments, your posture becomes a guidepost. Your ability to name what you know, acknowledge what you don't, and still take the next faithful step builds trust far more than confident declarations ever could. People don't need flawless leadership; they need anchored leadership.

Even when you feel uncertain inside, your commitment to clarity, care, and consistency tells a different story: one of resilience, responsibility, and presence. The fog may linger. The outcomes may remain unclear. But your willingness to lead anyway—to steer with honesty and heart—reminds those around you that uncertainty doesn't have to be paralyzing. It can become a space of possibility. And your quiet courage may be the reason others find the strength to keep moving forward, one step at a time.

> ▶ *Related Toolkit: Crisis Communication Toolkit (Appendix A)*

Daily Anchor for Leading Anyway

I accept that not every step will be clear. The fog does not mean I am lost. I move forward with what I know, trusting that clarity will meet me along the way. Leadership in the fog is not about waiting for perfect conditions; it is about the courage to keep walking with grace, wisdom, and patience.

> *Quietly or aloud, say after me:*
> **"I trust the process even when the path is unclear. I move forward with courage, knowing the fog will lift."**

🌐 CHAPTER 3 LEADERSHIP SNAPSHOT 🌐

 FRAMEWORK IN ACTION

This chapter directly supports three core components of the *Global Leadership Framework*:

Emotional Centering: By helping leaders stay grounded and avoid panic-based decision-making.

Communication and Trust: By showing how transparency and consistency build trust, even in uncertainty.

Cultural Coordination: By encouraging discernment and humility when urgency and noise compete for attention.

KEY LEADERSHIP TAKEAWAYS

- Leadership in crisis is about action rooted in presence—not perfection.
- Consistency builds trust faster than confidence.
- Discernment allows leaders to filter urgency from noise.
- Predictability provides emotional safety when certainty is unavailable.
- A clear process can steady others even when full answers are out of reach.

REFLECTIVE JOURNAL QUESTIONS

1. How do I usually respond when I don't have all the answers?

2. Where can I substitute performance with presence in my leadership?

3. What practices can help me distinguish real emergencies from loud distractions?

CULTURAL INSIGHT

In many collectivist and community-oriented cultures, discernment is valued more than speed. Leaders are expected to observe, listen, and align with the group's rhythm before responding. Chapter 3 affirms this by honoring the pause as a form of wisdom—reminding us that waiting to respond with clarity is not a delay, but rather depth.

USE THIS SECTION TO:

- Train field leaders on responsive decision-making during uncertainty
- Equip emerging leaders with language for naming "what we know" and "what comes next"
- Prepare school administrators, shelter managers, or NGO directors for high-pressure choices
- Reframe hesitation not as fear, but as a tool for more responsible action

Part II

Guiding Others
Through Chaos

In the absence of structure, your steadiness becomes the structure.

There comes a moment in every crisis when people look around for leadership—only to find none. The plan has failed. The system has stalled. The official voices have gone quiet. Yet the needs continue to rise.

This is the moment when your presence becomes the guidepost.

In this section, we move from internal grounding to external guidance. These chapters prepare you to lead others not through authority, but through clarity. You will learn how to communicate in ways that people can actually hear—especially in moments of panic. You will discover how to organize chaos without a title, how to create order amid uncertainty, and how to move others with steady purpose when roles are unclear and emotions are high.

You do not need to be the loudest voice in the room. You need to be the clearest. The calmest. The most grounded.

Because people do not rise to ideal conditions—they rise to the tone you set. That tone begins with how you guide them through the first wave of confusion, one breath, one decision, and one moment at a time.

Chapter 4

Speak So They Can Hear You

The Emotional Impact of Crisis Communication

After a disaster, people do not always remember the words you used. However, they remember the feeling your voice conveyed. Did it steady them or plunge them deeper into fear? Did it build trust or create confusion? In the fog of crisis, communication becomes more than mere information—it transforms into

"In chaos, communication is not just what you say—it's how you say it."

medicine. A grounding presence. A bridge between chaos and clarity.

Tone, timing, body language—even silence—carry emotional weight. A hurried explanation can feel like dismissal. A calm, steady tone can restore a sense of control. When uncertainty fills the air, your ability to regulate your own voice, presence, and message becomes a form of leadership in itself. People in crisis often read between the lines. They observe your face, your hands, and your pauses. They determine whether to trust based on how you speak, not just what you say.

This is why crisis communication must be emotionally intelligent. It's not about having the perfect script—it's about delivering every message with care, cultural sensitivity, and human dignity. In many cases, your words won't just inform—they will shape how people remember the moment. They may not recall your title, but they will remember if your presence helped them breathe.

Why Tone Matters More Than Words

Clear, emotionally attuned communication is one of the most powerful—yet underutilized—forms of care. In high-stress moments, the human brain loses some of its ability to process language. Neurologically, the brain shifts into survival mode. People perceive tone before they understand content. They respond more to rhythm than to logic. That's why lengthy explanations often backfire—and why a slow tone, steady cadence, and simple language are essential.

This holds true across languages, cultures, and settings. In a crowded emergency room in Jordan, a nurse's steady voice may do more to calm a panicked patient than any technical explanation. In a disaster shelter in the Caribbean, a volunteer's soothing tone may help a child fall asleep after days of displacement. In a rural village in Pakistan, the cadence of a community elder speaking calmly—even without all the facts—can settle an entire gathering. Tone bypasses the intellect and speaks directly to the nervous system. It communicates to people: You are safe. You are seen. You are not alone.

This is why emotionally intelligent leaders must become fluent not only in what they say—but also in how they say it. A leader who yells instructions may be technically correct but emotionally alienating. A leader who speaks too quickly may inadvertently convey urgency when steadiness is required. Conversely, a leader who slows down, centers their voice, and acknowledges the emotion in the room often achieves more with fewer words.

Tone becomes even more important in multilingual or cross-cultural settings, where meaning can be distorted in translation. However, emotion is rarely lost in tone. Calm is felt, care is recognized, and dignity is conveyed—even when words fall short. That is why tone is not just a

> "Clear words restore dignity. Rushed words destroy trust."

communication choice—it is a leadership strategy. In moments of crisis, it may be the most important tool you have.

Helping People Feel Safe Enough to Listen

Communication during a crisis isn't just about having all the answers; it's about helping people regain their footing. The most effective voices in disaster recovery do not dominate the conversation; they facilitate it. They make people feel seen, understood, and secure enough to listen.

In the aftermath of disruption, the nervous system is often in survival mode. People may struggle to process instructions, retain details, or even hear your words clearly. What they need first is a sense of psychological safety—an unspoken reassurance that they are not alone, not being judged, and not being rushed. Your tone, presence, and patience become anchors in the storm. Safety is not just physical; it is emotional. And without it, even the most accurate information can get lost in the noise.

To help people truly listen, you must first demonstrate that you are listening. Reflect their concerns. Validate their fears without inflaming them. Slow your speech if needed. Make space for silence. This kind of grounded communication is not weakness—it is leadership. Because when people feel emotionally safe, they regain the ability to think clearly, make decisions, and move forward with dignity.

Case Example
Storm Shelter in the UK

In Manchester, during a prolonged winter power outage, a community leader managed a school-turned-shelter. Rather than making bold claims, he began each update with, "Here's what we know, and here's what we're still learning." His quiet honesty, combined with steady body language, gave frightened families something to hold onto. It was not just his words that comforted them, but how he delivered them.

Cross-Cultural Sensitivity in Communication

This is especially critical in cross-cultural and multilingual environments, where leadership is not only about what you say, but also about how your words are received. In Port-au-Prince, Haiti, a firm and authoritative tone may convey strength and care. In an urban neighborhood of Johannesburg, that same tone might be interpreted as controlling or dismissive. In Nairobi, where English, Kiswahili, Sheng, and indigenous languages intersect, messages that overlook cultural nuances may inadvertently exclude key groups. In Sydney, directness may signal transparency and confidence; however, in rural Bangladesh, that same approach could be perceived as disrespectful, conflicting with values of humility and social harmony.

In many Indigenous communities across the Americas and the Pacific Islands, silence itself serves as a form of communication—a sign of respect, reflection, or trust-building. A rushed or overly directive tone in these contexts may seem impatient or overbearing. Similarly, in various Middle Eastern and Southeast Asian cultures, indirect phrasing helps preserve dignity. What may sound vague to a Western ear could be a deliberate effort to maintain harmony.

Global communication must extend well beyond translation. It should consider emotional nuance—the unspoken meanings expressed through gestures, pauses, tone, and pacing. What you intend to convey may not be what others perceive, and good intentions alone are insufficient if the delivery results in harm or confusion.

Questions to Ask Before Speaking

This is where emotional intelligence becomes essential. Before you speak—especially in a crisis—pause and ask yourself:

- **Who is this intended for?**
- **What are they carrying emotionally?**
- **What does this moment require—comfort, clarity, instruction, or stillness?**

- How can I speak in a way that honors both urgency and dignity?

"Your voice is a nervous system signal. Make it safe."

Your message should never focus on showcasing control or certainty. Instead, it should address the needs of the moment—making the complex feel manageable, acknowledging fears, and respecting people.

Clarity Without Platitudes

Speak in grounded, clear statements. Avoid overpromising or glossing over pain. "We are working to get food to this location by the end of the day" will always offer more comfort than "Everything's going to be okay." When people have lost homes, loved ones, or livelihoods, they do not need platitudes. They need precision, presence, and a plan.

In the wake of disaster, vague reassurances can feel hollow—or worse, dismissive. Well-meaning phrases like "Stay strong" or "It could've been worse" may unintentionally widen the gap between speaker and survivor. What people truly need in those moments is truth delivered with compassion. Clarity does not mean coldness; it means you respect the intelligence and emotional state of those receiving your words. It signals that you understand the weight of their reality—and are willing to meet it honestly.

Leadership communication during a crisis must connect the human and logistical aspects. It should validate grief while providing structure. Even if the complete solution is still developing, share what you do know. Be specific. Address what is happening now, not just what you hope will occur later. When survivors feel they are being communicated with transparently and respectfully, trust starts to take root—even in the most fragile conditions.

The Power of Stillness and Silence

Do not underestimate the power of silence. In trauma-informed communication, presence often conveys more clearly than words. A nurse in Lagos places a steady hand on a trembling shoulder. A teacher in Jakarta kneels beside a child, offering quiet reassurance with their eyes. A volunteer in Louisiana simply sits with a grieving elder, saying nothing yet refusing to leave. These moments of stillness express dignity, recognition, and respect—far more profoundly than any prepared speech ever could.

Across cultures, silence carries different meanings—yet in moments of crisis, it often becomes a universal language of care. In Japanese culture, silence may signal thoughtfulness and deference. In many Indigenous communities, it reflects respect and sacred listening. In Middle Eastern or Latin American contexts, silence can serve as an act of holding emotional space—allowing grief, fear, or confusion to breathe before attempting to soothe or solve.

Leaders sometimes feel pressured to fill the air with instructions, encouragement, or expertise. However, in high-stakes moments, people are not always looking for answers—they want to know they are not alone. Silence, when rooted in presence, becomes a powerful way to convey: I see you. I am with you. And I will not rush your pain.

Stillness also provides people with the space to discover their own strength. It fosters trust, creates an opportunity for clarity to emerge, and restores a sense of control for those who feel disoriented. Silence is not the absence of leadership—it is often its most courageous form.

Speak with Care and Intention

When you speak, do so thoughtfully. Allow your voice to be a steadying force. Let your words remind others that they are not invisible. Do not speak to perform. Speak to connect. Speak to guide. Speak with the awareness of someone who understands that every word, every gesture, and every tone can either deepen harm or help rebuild rapport.

In moments of crisis, your voice carries more than just information—it carries emotional weight. People are listening not only for updates but also for cues on whether they are safe, whether they matter, and whether they are truly seen. One careless phrase can fracture fragile trust, while one sincere word can offer calm amid chaos. This is why communication in disaster settings is not merely a skill—it is a responsibility.

Before you speak, pause. Ask yourself: Is what I'm about to say necessary? Is it true? Is it kind? Consider who is in the room, what they have endured, and what their silence might be trying to tell you. Speak with the intention to uplift, not impress; to steady, not spotlight. When your words come from a place of humility, presence, and care, they become more than language—they become leadership.

Building and Rebuilding Trust

Trust is fragile during a disaster. Avoid making promises you cannot keep. If plans change, communicate that clearly. If people express anger, listen without becoming defensive. If you are uncertain, acknowledge it. Leadership is not about appearing in control—it is about being genuine, dependable, and grounded in care.

In post-crisis environments, trust is not granted—it is earned moment by moment. Communities may grieve, feel disoriented, or remain skeptical due to past experiences with broken systems or failed responses. In these spaces, every interaction becomes part of the trust-building process. The way you show up—the consistency of your presence, the honesty in your voice, and the respect in your actions—matters more than titles or timelines.

Rebuilding trust also means acknowledging when it has been damaged and having the courage to repair it. A sincere apology, a transparent update, or simply staying to answer difficult questions can go further than rehearsed talking points. Trust is established when people feel that you are with them, not above them; when they see that your care is unconditional; and when your words match your actions, especially when no one is watching.

In disaster leadership, trust serves as the invisible infrastructure. Without it, even the most well-resourced plans can collapse. With it, communities discover the strength to move forward—even through the rubble.

Inclusive Language as a Leadership Practice

Across the globe, language carries histories of harm and healing. In every region, there are phrases that silence and words that dignify. Inclusive communication is not about being perfect; it is about being conscious—of power, of pain, of presence. It involves recognizing who has been excluded from conversations in the past and choosing to speak in ways that bring them back in.

Language is never neutral. Words shape perception, and perception shapes response. In crisis settings, where emotions run high and identities are deeply felt, the words you choose can either open a door or reinforce a wall. Inclusive language means saying "we" instead of "they," recognizing varied family structures, using gender-respectful terminology, and avoiding colonial, ableist, or dismissive language— whether in speech, signage, or written updates.

But beyond vocabulary, inclusive language is a practice of emotional attunement. It requires listening to how individuals identify themselves, their struggles, and their communities—and adjusting your language to honor that respect. It means inquiring, not assuming. It means updating your terminology as culture evolves. Most importantly, it means recognizing that language is a bridge—not just to improved communication, but to greater equity and healing.

When leaders choose their words carefully, they do more than inform; they affirm dignity, create space, and model the kind of world we are striving to rebuild—one where every voice has value.

> ## Case Example
> ## Trauma-Informed School Leadership
> ## in Manchester
>
> After extended lockdowns and school closures in Manchester, student anxiety and behavioral disruptions surged upon reopening. A local secondary school principal collaborated with counselors to create trauma-informed classroom adjustments: structured morning check-ins, quiet spaces for emotional regulation, and personalized support for students grieving family losses. Teachers received brief resilience coaching to help de-escalate emotional outbursts with calm authority. While academic gaps persisted as a challenge, the school's emotionally grounded leadership approach restored stability, belonging, and emotional safety for hundreds of returning students.

The Quiet Mayor of the Mountain Town

The cameras arrived during the first week. National networks broadcast images of collapsed bridges, flooded streets, and families airlifted from rooftops. Aid poured in, relief organizations set up tents, and politicians showed up for photographs. However, as the weeks passed and the news cycle moved on, the cameras departed.

But the town still remained.

Nestled in the mountains and cut off from major supply chains, this community faced a difficult road to recovery. Months after the initial disaster, homes remained damaged, roads were still blocked, and businesses stayed closed. The mayor, a soft-spoken man in his early fifties, lacked a background in emergency management; he had been a teacher before transitioning to public service. However, in the absence of national attention, he became the steady force his people needed.

Every morning, he walked through town—not with a television crew, but with a notebook. He inquired with shop owners about their needs. He organized local volunteers to clear debris in areas where federal crews had not yet arrived. He collaborated with neighboring towns to exchange supplies and secure temporary schooling for displaced children. At night, he returned home to read every regulation, grant application, and recovery procedure he could find.

Months passed, turning into years. Gradually, the town started to rebuild. Not flawlessly. Not rapidly. But consistently.

Long after the cameras have forgotten the storm, this leader recognized something essential: recovery is not a headline. It is a discipline. It requires leading after the storm, when the world's attention has moved on, but your people still need you to be present.

2018 Snapshot: When the Sea Struck Twice (Indonesia, Sulawesi Earthquake & Tsunami)

In 2018, the island of Sulawesi in Indonesia experienced a powerful earthquake with a magnitude of 7.5. Minutes later, a tsunami followed, crashing into coastal communities and erasing entire neighborhoods in mere moments. Streets that once housed homes, markets, and schools became unrecognizable. In the aftermath of the disaster, local teachers, youth leaders, and healthcare workers acted swiftly to set up makeshift shelters for survivors.

With limited supplies and communication lines down, they organized food distributions, coordinated missing persons lists, and cared for frightened children separated from their families. As night fell, elders gathered groups to sing familiar songs—soft melodies that carried cultural memory and comfort into crowded tents. Faith leaders offered prayers not only for those who were lost but also for the strength to care for those still standing. Their leadership, rooted in cultural resilience and quiet courage, became the first stabilizing force in a community struggling to breathe beneath the weight of sudden loss.

2025 Snapshot: When the Sky Breaks Open

The year 2025 brought an unsettling wave of aviation disasters. Multiple commercial planes plummeted from the sky across continents—mechanical failures, communication breakdowns, and catastrophic malfunctions that shook public trust worldwide. Behind the headlines were teams of first responders, air traffic controllers, grief counselors, and airline leaders who bore the weight of the immediate aftermath. Families gathered in airport waiting rooms, desperate for news. While the world watched the unfolding tragedies, quiet teams worked tirelessly—holding the hands of survivors, managing international coordination, and delivering devastating news with dignity. In these moments, leadership became less about titles and more about human presence in unimaginable grief.

Closing Insight: Speak to Settle, Not to Impress

You do not need to be eloquent. You need to be honest, calm, clear, and human. In moments of crisis, people are not listening for brilliance—they are listening for truth wrapped in care. Speak in a way that opens rather than closes, includes rather than excludes, and calms rather than startles. Speak in a way that shows people they matter—not just because you're addressing them, but because you took the time to understand how to communicate with them.

Leadership communication is not about flawless delivery; it is about emotional presence. It is the quiet steadiness that says, "I am here. I see you. We will move forward together." When you lead with this kind of clarity and humility, your words do more than convey information—they transmit safety, dignity, and belonging. That is grounding communication. That is leadership that heals.

Because in the aftermath of disaster, what people most need is not someone who sounds impressive; they need someone who sounds like they care. Someone who chooses words with empathy. Someone who slows down long enough to connect. And someone who knows that healing often begins—not with action—but with how we speak.

▶ *Related Toolkit: Crisis Communication Toolkit (Appendix A)*

Daily Anchor for Leading Anyway

My words are a tool of leadership. I release the need to force or demand. Instead, I choose language that opens hearts, clarifies intentions, and allows truth to land where it is needed. I honor both the message and the moment. When I speak, I am not only heard — I am understood.

> *Quietly or aloud, say after me:*
> **"I speak with clarity, respect, and wisdom. My words create understanding and open doors."**

🌐 CHAPTER 4 LEADERSHIP SNAPSHOT 🌐

 FRAMEWORK IN ACTION

This chapter supports two vital components of the *Global Leadership Framework*:

Communication and Trust: By emphasizing clarity, compassion, and cultural attunement in spoken leadership.

Cultural Coordination: By promoting inclusive, trauma-aware, and culturally respectful language during crisis communication.

KEY LEADERSHIP TAKEAWAYS

- The tone of your voice is often remembered longer than the words.
- Crisis communication must be grounded, not performative.
- Inclusive language builds dignity and psychological safety.
- Clarity is more powerful than false reassurance—avoid platitudes.
- Communication that calms is a form of leadership in itself.

REFLECTIVE JOURNAL QUESTIONS

1. When I speak in difficult moments, do I aim to calm or to control?

2. What language habits or phrases could unintentionally exclude or diminish others?

3. How can I create a communication style that both informs and reassures?

CULTURAL INSIGHT

In regions affected by colonial trauma, war, or displacement, words carry profound histories. Language that may seem neutral in one culture can evoke pain in another. Chapter 4 affirms the global importance of emotionally intelligent speech—where healing begins not in eloquence, but in awareness, humility, and care.

USE THIS SECTION TO:

- Train leaders, educators, or coordinators in trauma-informed public communication

- Support media spokespeople or aid workers delivering community updates
- Audit your team's language habits for inclusivity, clarity, and emotional resonance
- Facilitate multilingual or multicultural team discussions around tone, trust, and interpretation

Chapter 5

Step Forward Anyway

The Call to Lead Without Being Asked

Disasters rarely inquire about who's in charge. They do not pause for titles, organizational charts, or formal approvals. They tear through systems, disrupt hierarchies, and leave communities searching for someone—anyone—willing to act. Often, the individual who steps forward is not the most senior, the most trained, or the most equipped. It is simply someone who cannot wait any longer.

> "Leadership in disaster isn't granted. It's chosen."

These moments demand leadership rooted not in authority, but in courage. A neighbor who organizes a meal drop-off. A teacher who opens the school gates before officials arrive. A young person who begins translating urgent instructions for elders. This type of leadership is not assigned—it is activated. It emerges from necessity, compassion, and an unwillingness to let silence have the final word.

Leading without being asked means recognizing the moment for what it is: an invitation to serve, to steady, and to help others breathe more easily. It may not come with applause. It may not feel glamorous, but it is sacred work. This is how communities survive—not by waiting for permission, but by answering the call to care out loud.

Emergent Leadership Around the World

Around the globe, this type of leadership arises quietly. A teenager directs traffic away from a collapsed road in rural Kenya. A woman in New Orleans organizes a food line after the levees break. A community elder in Samoa calls out instructions because the silence is too heavy to bear. This is emergent leadership—and it saves lives.

It is not formalized. It is not always recognized. Yet, it exists everywhere—in refugee camps, in flooded villages, in earthquake zones, and on the front steps of homes that no longer stand. Emergent leaders are those who notice what needs to be done and start, without waiting for applause or direction. They move instinctively, anchored in care and rooted in their responsibility to those around them.

What connects these leaders across countries and cultures is not their position—it is their presence. They are often the first to comfort, to organize, to speak, or simply to stand still when others are unraveling. Their actions ripple outward, restoring a sense of order, dignity, and possibility in the midst of uncertainty. In times of crisis, these unsung leaders become the heartbeat of recovery—proving that leadership is not reserved for the designated, but awakened in those who dare to respond.

Case Example
Rural Response in Kerala, India

During the 2018 floods in Kerala, a local fisherman used his boat to rescue dozens of people, including those stranded on rooftops. With no official guidance, he navigated the flooded streets based on memory and instinct. Eventually, other volunteers followed his lead, forming one of the earliest coordinated responses in the area. His courage filled a leadership void before formal authorities arrived.

Case Example
Drought Response in Northern Kenya

During a prolonged drought, local women leaders organized water distribution stations powered by solar energy. Despite resource scarcity and the absence of formal aid, these women coordinated herders, shared childcare duties, and protected vulnerable elders—all while navigating tribal tensions. Their resilience stemmed not from external motivation but from community legacy and spiritual responsibility.

Case Example
Spain – After the Fire, After the Flood

In 2022 and 2023, Spain faced consecutive environmental crises that challenged the resilience of its regions and leadership systems. First came the record-breaking wildfires in Zamora and Extremadura, intensified by heatwaves and drought. Then, just months later, flash floods hit Valencia and parts of Catalonia, displacing hundreds and disrupting regional infrastructure.

What stood out was how municipal leaders, civil protection units, and neighborhood associations in Spain activated multiple layers of response. In rural communities, farmers converted their irrigation systems into firebreaks. In urban areas, community centers turned into distribution hubs for supplies and shelter.

However, it was the continuity of care during crises that defined true leadership. One school in Valencia, which had served as a shelter for fire recovery, reopened months later as a flood response site—coordinated by the same group of teachers, clergy,

"You don't need a title to bring structure to chaos."

and youth leaders. Their model emphasized continuity, local trust, and collective presence.

Spain's evolving coordination model reminds us that resilience is not just about bouncing back; it is about adapting through waves of disruption, using emotional and cultural intelligence to meet each moment uniquely.

Case Example
Barcelona, Spain – Coordinating Calm
During the 2017 Terror Attack

In August 2017, a van plowed into crowds on Las Ramblas in Barcelona, killing 13 people and injuring over 100 in a coordinated terrorist attack. What followed was not only a swift emergency response but also an extraordinary demonstration of local coordination. City authorities, emergency services, mental health professionals, and civil society groups worked together within hours to establish multilingual crisis lines, family reunification centers, and public messaging that emphasized unity over fear.

Barcelona's response was particularly effective due to the rapid activation of neighborhood networks already trained in community response. Street-level leaders, including teachers, clergy, and local volunteers, guided tourists to safety, calmed panicked families, and translated emergency messages for non-Spanish speakers. In the days that followed, thousands gathered peacefully in the city center under the banner "No Tinc Por" ("I'm not afraid"), a phrase that became both a public statement and a psychological anchor.

Their coordinated calm did not erase the pain; rather, it transformed it. The leaders who emerged, many without titles or formal authority, embodied the essence of community-centered crisis coordination: clarity, compassion, and collective care.

When Local Leadership Becomes the Lifeline

Disasters do not merely test infrastructure—they test relationships. In Spain, as in many regions around the globe, it was not federal agencies or outside organizations that first restored stability. It was the local teacher who transformed a classroom into a shelter. It was the neighborhood leader who redirected the community WhatsApp group to organize food pickups. It was the volunteer firefighter who remained awake for three consecutive days checking basements for flood victims.

These are not abstract acts of heroism. They are tangible examples of decentralized, responsive leadership—where ordinary individuals respond with extraordinary clarity. The crisis did not create their leadership; it unveiled it.

When national systems are overwhelmed or delayed, local leaders set the emotional, cultural, and strategic tone. The Spain example reminds us: it is not always about titles—it is about presence. It is about who listens first, speaks last, and shows up between the shock and the solution.

If you are that person in your community, your leadership may never make headlines. But it will make healing possible.

The Emotional Weight of Leading Without Permission

Emergent leadership arises from necessity, not designation. It is not about authority; it is about response. However, stepping into leadership without being asked carries emotional weight. You may feel exposed, questioned, or overlooked. You may fear overstepping roles or disrupting existing systems. These concerns are particularly valid in environments where hierarchy, age, gender, or class significantly shape expectations of who is "allowed" to lead.

> "Authority is not position—it's presence under pressure."

61

When the moment calls for you, yet lives are in flux and systems are slow to respond, the question shifts from "Who am I to lead?" to "Who am I not to?" Crisis leadership is not about ego; it is about action grounded in care.

This type of leadership does not require a badge. It demands courage, clarity, and the willingness to step forward even when the path is unclear. It is not about taking control; it's about showing up, being the steady voice amid the chaos, and coordinating what you can with what you have until more help arrives.

Case Example
Informal Coordination in the Philippines

In the aftermath of Typhoon Haiyan, a teenager in Tacloban City began organizing food lines using scraps of cardboard and a whistle. He had no official role, but his presence helped bring order to an overwhelmed evacuation site. Relief teams later reported that his actions likely prevented stampedes and panic.

Case Example
Neighborhood Leadership in Lahaina, Hawaii

During the 2023 wildfires in Lahaina, a local store manager utilized his warehouse to shelter families and distribute supplies. Lacking cell service and electricity, he coordinated with neighbors on foot, writing down names and needs on a large whiteboard. His swift, localized leadership stabilized hundreds of people within the first 48 hours.

Why It Still Matters Without a Title

In many parts of the world—rural villages in India, inner-city neighborhoods in the United States, flood zones in Australia, or earthquake-affected areas in Turkey—the official response lags. Communication lines break down, and resources come to a halt. In that gap, it is often ordinary people who step into leadership. Not because they were trained for it, but because they are close enough to the need to feel it deeply.

These leaders are not always welcomed warmly. They may encounter challenges, face dismissal, or be blamed when things go wrong. The journey of emergent leadership can feel isolating. It often involves managing resistance from those who don't see you as "in charge," or navigating unspoken power dynamics without clear guidelines. Nonetheless, the presence of someone willing to act with intention rather than panic can change the course of an entire recovery.

Action with Intention, Not Panic

But mere movement does not constitute leadership. The world doesn't require more reactions—it requires more regulation. Acting out of panic creates confusion. Acting with purpose fosters trust.

So ask yourself in the moment: What can I do right now to bring about clarity, calm, and care? Perhaps it means establishing a common meeting point. Maybe it involves checking in on vulnerable neighbors or organizing the distribution of supplies. Perhaps it simply means being the one who listens—who holds the chaos and helps translate it into the next step.

Leadership That Listens and Includes

Leadership does not always resemble command. Sometimes it involves staying when others leave. Sometimes it means waiting until others are ready to move with you. Sometimes it requires giving others the microphone, even when your voice could lead.

There is no perfect formula for leading when structure collapses. However, there are values to embrace: transparency, humility, and community trust. You can choose to empower instead of control. You can choose to co-lead rather than direct. You can model honesty, acknowledge what you do not know, and still present the next steady action.

2023 Snapshot: The Quake Without Borders (Turkey-Syria Earthquake)

In February 2023, a 7.8 magnitude earthquake struck the border region of Turkey and Syria, collapsing thousands of buildings within minutes. Entire apartment blocks were flattened while families slept. Rescue teams faced freezing temperatures, damaged roads, and overwhelmed hospitals. Yet, before official teams could even arrive, neighbors became the first responders.

Fathers, brothers, teenagers, and grandmothers dug through the rubble with bare hands and makeshift tools, listening for faint cries beneath concrete slabs. In northern Syria, where ongoing conflict had already weakened infrastructure for years, local aid workers operated without reliable equipment or formal coordination. Their leadership was defined not by job titles or disaster protocols but by presence, courage, and the refusal to abandon those still trapped beneath the ruins. During moments when government systems stalled, it was ordinary people who carried extraordinary weight.

Closing Insight: Step Forward Anyway

This is not about improvisation for the sake of movement. It is about responsive leadership—anchored in emotional presence, cultural awareness, and a genuine commitment to those around you. You may never receive an official invitation to lead. But you will feel the moment when the world quietly asks for your courage.

There may be no applause, no title, and no formal permission. And still—there will be people watching, hoping someone will speak, guide, or simply care out loud. Let that be enough. Step forward when the moment calls for it—not to prove yourself, but to protect what matters: safety, dignity, and connection.

Sometimes, what a community needs most is not another directive or chain of command. It needs a single steady voice to shift the energy—from panic to possibility, from fear to focus, from confusion to clarity. It needs one act of grounded care to move people from disorganization to collective strength.

Wherever you are in the world, remember this: You do not need permission to be a calming presence. You do not need a title to lead with integrity. Leadership begins when we decide to show up—with clarity, with compassion, and with the courage to serve anyway.

▶ *Related Toolkit: Leadership Log Template (Appendix E)*

Daily Anchor for Leading Anyway

Leadership requires motion. Even when uncertainty whispers and fear tries to stall my progress, I choose to move forward. Courage is not the absence of hesitation — it is the decision to continue stepping through it. I give myself permission to act without waiting for perfect readiness. My leadership grows with each step I take.

> *Quietly or aloud, say after me:*
> **"I step forward with courage. Progress is made one decision at a time. I am in motion."**

🌐 CHAPTER 5 LEADERSHIP SNAPSHOT 🌐

 FRAMEWORK IN ACTION

This chapter reinforces three key pillars of the *Global Leadership Framework*:

Emotional Centering: By encouraging self-trust and internal stability when plans fall apart.

Adaptive Leadership: By modeling how to lead through disruption, ambiguity, and real-time recalibration.

Cultural Coordination: By acknowledging the need to adapt plans across contexts, communities, and cultural expectations.

 KEY LEADERSHIP TAKEAWAYS

▷ Leadership does not always follow a script—and that's not failure.
▷ Flexibility with structure builds resilience and collective trust.
▷ Emotional regulation supports better improvisation under pressure.
▷ Clinging to the plan may cause more harm than adapting with care.
▷ Authenticity matters more than control during times of disruption.

REFLECTIVE JOURNAL QUESTIONS

1. How should I react when the plan no longer works?

2. What anchors me when I feel lost or uncertain as a leader?

3. How can I honor the need for both structure and spontaneity in my role?

CULTURAL INSIGHT

Many Indigenous and global community leadership models rely on responsive wisdom rather than rigid planning. Wisdom keepers, elders, or local guides are often trusted to interpret evolving conditions instead of enforcing static solutions. Chapter 5 affirms that adaptive leadership is not a weakness; it is a cultural strength found in collaborative, relational systems worldwide.

USE THIS SECTION TO:

- Coach leaders during high-pressure, rapidly changing environments
- Support team debriefs after pivots, setbacks, or natural disruptions
- Train emerging leaders in flexibility, discernment, and emotional presence
- Reframe chaos not as a loss of control, but as a call for collective creativity

Chapter 6

Organizing the Chaos

GLOBAL REALITY CHECK
NATURE NO LONGER WAITS

In June 2025, southern Europe ignited. Wildfires swept across Greece, France, Spain, and Italy during an unrelenting heatwave, with temperatures soaring past 40 degrees Celsius. In Chios, Greece, entire villages were evacuated as flames engulfed the hillsides and firefighting teams raced to contain the spread. Days later, highways near Athens were shut down as fires crept dangerously close to densely populated areas and international tourist zones. These were not isolated incidents—they were warnings.

Wildfires are no longer seasonal anomalies. They are alarm bells in a climate-adjacent leadership reality. As extreme weather events become more frequent, they expose more than ecological vulnerabilities. They reveal cracks in infrastructure, fragile inter-agency communication, and the need for emotionally clear leadership under pressure.

Coordinating during chaos now requires a deeper kind of foresight. Leaders are no lon-

> "In the absence of structure, your presence becomes the plan."

ger organizing around fixed timelines—they are organizing around uncertainty itself. Nature has stripped away the illusion of predictability. Monsoons arrive early. Wildfires burn out of season. Drought turns farmland into fractured terrain. And through it all, leadership must respond without freezing, deflecting, or disappearing.

In climate-driven emergencies, communities do not only need resources—they need presence. They need leaders who can communicate across systems, who can ground others emotionally, and who understand that clarity is its own kind of emergency aid. As the planet continues to shift, the leaders who thrive will be those who can organize not just tools and people, but tone, timing, and trust. The more the natural world changes, the more emotional sustainability becomes a leadership imperative.

Framework in Action: Coordinating in a Climate-Changed World

In climate-driven disasters, coordination must evolve beyond rigid command structures. During the 2025 Mediterranean wildfires, miscommunication between local municipalities, firefighting units, and national agencies caused delays that lost valuable time. By contrast, in Kerala, India, annual flood response simulations involve school principals, religious leaders, transit workers, and village elders in joint planning and practice. These systems work not because they are perfect, but because they are practiced—and emotionally grounded.

The Global Leadership Framework emphasizes that coordination is not about controlling every outcome. It is about aligning people through shared clarity, trust, and readiness, even when the environment is unpredictable. True coordination includes listening, emotional regulation, and cross-sector humility.

"Delegation is not losing control—it's creating stability."

Reflective Journal Prompt

Think of a recent crisis your region faced. Was it treated as a surprise or as a recurring possibility?

What might change if your leadership community organized around patterns of emerging chaos rather than waiting for formal declarations of disaster?

Collective Model Highlight

In parts of southern Africa, traditional fire management includes controlled seasonal burns, coordinated by elders, farmers, and ecological stewards. These practices reduce wildfire risk by honoring cycles of nature and community cooperation. Leadership in this context is relational, rhythmic, and reciprocal—a reminder that when we listen to the land, we lead more wisely.

From Motion to Meaning: Why Coordination Matters

After a disaster, movement is everywhere. People rush, voices rise, and hands reach for anything useful. However, motion does not equal direction. Without coordination, even the most sincere efforts risk spiraling into disorder.

This is where leadership must shift from instinct to structure.

When there is no visible command center, you become the anchor. When there is no written plan, you become the compass. However, organizing chaos is not about seizing control; it's about creating space. Space for others to breathe. Space for people to contribute their strengths. Space for the community to begin remembering what stability feels like.

In every region of the world, there are cultural norms regarding how leadership is expressed—some vocal, some quiet. Effective coordination honors these differences. It does not bulldoze through urgency; it listens, observes, and then aligns people toward shared action. Whether you're organizing food lines in Haiti, evacuation points in the Philippines, or supply stations in a flooded Texas town, the principle remains: meaning emerges when motion is met with intention.

When coordination is handled with care, it does more than reduce chaos. It restores dignity. It helps people reclaim their agency in a time that has stripped them of control. It tells communities: you are not alone—we are moving through this, together, with purpose.

Clarity Before Action

Early responses are filled with competing demands. Medical needs pull in one direction, while missing supplies pull in another. Families search for safety as volunteers seek purpose. Without structure, the emotional and physical toll multiplies. Leaders who try to solve everything at once quickly burn out—and often take their teams with them.

That's why the initial step of coordination is not action—it's clarity. Not perfect solutions, but a grounded assessment:

- What is going on right now?
- What is the most urgent matter?
- Who is present, and what can they actually accomplish?

These questions do not require precision. They require presence. And presence starts with listening.

The Emotional Side of Logistics

Field coordination is never merely logistical; it's also emotional. You often navigate a mix of personalities: overwhelmed parents, eager teenagers, elders dealing with grief, and volunteers who have seen too much. Some are ready to serve, while others are immobilized by trauma—and many are experiencing both. Coordination is not about perfect control of people—it's about cultivating a rhythm that others can join.

Behind every task is a nervous system. Behind every delay or misstep is someone who may be hungry, sleep-deprived, grieving, or quietly holding fear. If you approach logistics as purely mechanical—who does what, where, and when—you risk overlooking the very human dynamics that make or break a coordinated effort. Emotional awareness enables you to notice when someone needs a break, when tensions are rising, or when a moment of recognition could re-energize a fatigued team.

In communities around the world, this emotional layer of coordination often falls to the unspoken leaders—the grandmothers who gently redirect conflict, the youth who notice when someone has withdrawn, and the neighbors who bring food without being asked. These quiet interventions carry as much weight as any supply chain. They shape morale, prevent collapse, and restore dignity.

Effective coordination, then, requires not only structure but also empathy embedded in the system. It means creating space for both action and emotion. A logistics plan that succeeds on paper but exhausts people in practice is not sustainable. However, when you lead with both clarity and compassion, you create conditions that allow people to contribute fully—not just as workers but as whole human beings. That is where real resilience takes root.

Setting the Tone: Calm Creates Stability

That tempo starts with you. In high-stress environments, your tone becomes a leadership tool. When a leader remains calm, others often begin to feel calm as well. A steady voice helps reduce emotional reactions. A consistent rhythm allows people to breathe and feel more secure. Most people want to help—but they need to feel emotionally safe to do so. Your presence and demeanor influence the emotional atmosphere of the group.

This kind of emotional steadiness is not accidental—it is practiced. It results from leaders choosing regulation over reaction, breath over urgency, and clarity over noise. Around the world, in shelters, field hospitals, and coordination centers, this principle holds true: people mirror what they sense. If you project groundedness, others will begin to adjust their pace, tone, and even their outlook in response to you.

Calm does not mean passivity; it does not imply ignoring urgency or downplaying pain. Instead, it involves creating the conditions for thoughtful action. In emotionally charged moments, people often forget what was said, but they remember how they felt in your presence. Were they rushed or reassured? Overwhelmed or supported? Belittled or empowered?

By intentionally setting the emotional tone, you create a ripple effect. You shift the energy in the room, allowing others to transition from panic to participation. In doing so, you cultivate an environment where true recovery—emotional, logistical, and communal—can begin. Calm is not merely a trait; it is a leadership choice that, when practiced consistently, becomes a shared rhythm for others to follow.

Delegation as Dignity

Many leaders still struggle with delegation. The instinct to do everything oneself—especially under high pressure—is common. It can feel faster, safer, even noble to shoulder the weight alone. But in reality, doing it all yourself is not sustainable—and it often signals to others that their contributions are unnecessary or not trusted. In high-stakes environments, this unspoken message can unintentionally disempower the very people who are ready to serve.

True coordination requires allowing others to step in—even if they do it differently than you would. Delegation is not merely a logistics strategy; it is a human affirmation. It communicates, I see your value. I trust your judgment. You matter here. It turns helpers into stakeholders and transforms passive waiting into purposeful action.

In culturally diverse contexts, where roles are often shaped by age, gender, or hierarchy, intentional delegation can shift dynamics in powerful ways. It can create space for youth voices in elder-led communities or amplify women's leadership in traditionally male-dominated environments. It fosters moments where dignity is restored through action—where a grandmother organizing meal distribution or a teenager managing supply records feels their worth reflected in real responsibility.

When individuals are given genuine responsibility, they rise. They discover purpose. They feel less like bystanders and more like contributors. In the fragile aftermath of disaster, that sense of contribution can prove as healing as any material resource. Delegation, at its best, is not merely about assigning tasks; it is about inviting people back to their own agency—one clear role, one small act of trust at a time.

Case Example
Community Activation in California

After the Paradise wildfires in California, a local librarian transformed her branch into a coordination center. She assigned tasks based on energy and capacity rather than status—young adults helped guide people to shelters, while older adults assisted in tracking the names of missing residents. Her ability to create structure with available resources helped stabilize hundreds of displaced families.

Case Example
Mudslide Coordination in Colombia

In Mocoa, Colombia, after the devastating 2017 mudslides, local shopkeepers and teachers quickly became de facto first responders. Lacking formal training, they organized safe zones for children, secured clean water from surviving wells, and worked with local clergy to create temporary sleeping areas inside churches. Although national agencies eventually arrived, these early community leaders stabilized hundreds of families during the crucial first 48 hours. Their intimate knowledge of the terrain, kinship networks, and language patterns enabled resources to flow efficiently even amid destruction.

Case Example
Cyclone Idai Recovery in Mozambique

After Cyclone Idai devastated central Mozambique in 2019, local fishermen became first responders in the flooded city of Beira. Using small boats, they ferried stranded families to safety while coordinating by word of mouth when telecommunications failed. Women's cooperatives quickly organized food sharing and makeshift childcare zones as displaced families crowded into schools and churches. These grassroots leadership networks filled critical gaps long before international aid could arrive — reminding responders that local knowledge often provides the most immediate solutions.

Case Example
Earthquake Response in Uzbekistan

In 2023, a 6.3 magnitude earthquake struck near Namangan, Uzbekistan, causing damage to hundreds of homes and public buildings. Without immediate national deployment, local mahalla leaders—longstanding neighborhood elders—swiftly activated response networks. They coordinated access to food storage, identified displaced families, and negotiated shared housing agreements among relatives to prevent overcrowded shelters. By blending cultural norms of hospitality with rapid community coordination, they minimized secondary trauma while awaiting external aid. Their leadership reflected the power of deeply embedded community trust structures commonly found throughout Central Asia.

Match Energy, Not Just Skill

Delegation works best when it's aligned with energy and availability, rather than merely skill. In Mozambique, a teenager familiar with the terrain helped guide water deliveries to isolated families. In Puerto Rico, a grandmother tracked missing persons by simply listening to conversations and noting names. A local business owner in Port-au-Prince converted his storefront into a makeshift resource center. Coordination isn't about assigning based on rank; it's about unlocking the possibilities with the people you have.

When leaders align responsibilities with the natural rhythm, intuition, and willingness of those present, they create momentum that is sustainable and empowering. In high-stress environments, people often surprise themselves with what they are capable of—if given the chance. A quiet teenager may become the most reliable communicator. A retired teacher may manage logistics with precision honed over decades in classrooms. By recognizing and affirming each person's unique energy—not just their résumé—leaders encourage ownership, build morale, and foster a collective response that honors everyone's capacity to contribute, regardless of how unexpected the source.

Responsiveness Over Rigidity

But even the best plans can fray. Misunderstandings arise. Emotions flare. Systems fail. That's part of the work. Effective field leadership requires responsiveness rather than rigidity.

Sometimes, this means reassigning someone with care—acknowledging that emotional overwhelm is just as real as physical fatigue. Other times, it may involve prioritizing rest over performance, allowing people to pause instead of pushing through. At times, it means resolving a conflict not through control, but through presence—by choosing to listen fully before responding.

Rigid leadership often stems from fear—fear of losing control, of appearing weak, of not meeting expectations. However, in the field, where pressure runs high and predictability is rare, rigidity can shatter morale faster than the crisis itself. Responsive leadership, by contrast, breathes flexibility into the moment. It says: "I see what is needed now, not just what was planned before."

This doesn't mean lowering standards or abandoning structure. It means adapting with wisdom. It means knowing when to shift course, when to soften the tone, and when to step in—not to overpower, but to steady the team.

Leadership in these spaces is not about demanding perfection. It's about cultivating trust in motion—through small pivots, humble recalibrations, and the courage to care in real time.

Case Example
Flood Coordination in the Eastern Cape, South Africa

In a South African township affected by flash floods, a high school principal utilized her classroom roster as a coordination grid. By organizing students and families based on neighborhood proximity, she established a decentralized system of daily check-ins throughout the community. What began as a teacher's instinct rapidly evolved into the backbone of the local response effort—allowing vulnerable residents to be accounted for, supplies to be shared, and neighborhoods to stabilize while formal aid teams mobilized.

Case Example
Mudslide Response in Guatemala

In 2015, a catastrophic mudslide swept through the town of El Cambray II in Guatemala, burying homes and entire families within seconds. While formal rescue teams rushed to the scene, it was often neighbors—armed with shovels, ropes, and little else—who first began pulling survivors from the debris. Women set up makeshift childcare zones as parents searched for their loved ones. Local pastors coordinated food deliveries from nearby villages, while elders provided prayers and emotional support to grieving families. Long after foreign aid departed, these grassroots leaders remained—helping to rebuild not only structures but also trust, dignity, and community stability.

Navigating External Aid: Be the Bridge

If you are collaborating with NGOs, government agencies, or international aid teams, the complexity increases. These organizations often introduce systems—sometimes helpful, sometimes cumbersome. You may feel pressure to concede or instinctively resist.

Instead, be the bridge. You understand the community. You grasp the culture. You know what's needed right now. Use that insight. Advocate clearly. Coordinate with respect. And when frameworks clash, stand your ground with steadiness, not hostility.

> "Leadership isn't doing it all—it's making clarity contagious."

The Shelter Worker Who Never Left

The gymnasium had been transformed overnight. Cots lined the basketball court. Rows of tables held bottled water, canned goods, and first-aid supplies. Volunteers moved swiftly, checking names, distributing blankets, and trying to bring a small sense of order to the disoriented families arriving through the doors.

Among the volunteers was Angela, a local resident who was not affiliated with any official organization. She came the day after the storm because her own home was spared, while many others were damaged. Initially, she thought she would help for a few days—serving meals, organizing supplies, and offering comfort to strangers whose lives had been turned upside down.

But the days became weeks.

The official agencies rotated teams in and out. Some organizations came for short-term deployments, while others remained for extended periods. The media arrived and departed. But Angela stayed put.

She learned the names of the children sleeping on cots. She sat with elderly evacuees who had no family nearby. She gently mediated when tensions flared between families sharing close quarters. She became the quiet, familiar presence in a room that often felt like everything comforting had been taken away.

What Angela understood instinctively was that recovery isn't just about logistics; it's about presence. While formal leadership structures coordinated funding and policy, it was the consistent, daily presence of people like Angela that held the emotional fabric of the shelter together.

Sometimes leadership is not announced. Sometimes it simply stays.

2025 Snapshot: The Heat That Would Not Break

As 2025 unfolded, record-breaking heatwaves swept across continents, shattering temperature records in already vulnerable places. Cities like Phoenix, Delhi, Riyadh, and parts of southern Europe endured brutal stretches where temperatures soared beyond human tolerance. Power grids strained, hospitals overflowed, and elderly citizens collapsed in homes without air conditioning. In this invisible disaster, leadership emerged quietly: school principals converted buildings into cooling centers; community leaders coordinated water deliveries; faith leaders opened sanctuaries to shelter families. These were not dramatic moments captured on breaking news, but sustained, daily leadership that kept communities alive one degree at a time.

Closing Insight: Rhythm Builds Coherence

Ultimately, field coordination is not about managing every detail. It is about helping others move in the same direction—not because they were told to, but because they trust the rhythm you've created. This rhythm fosters coherence, and coherence brings calm.

You may never receive recognition for this role; field coordinators rarely do. However, your impact will resonate in every moment that runs more smoothly than it otherwise could have, in every parent reunited, in every meal that arrives on time, and in every moment where, against all odds, people remember what it felt like to be seen, supported, and part of something steady.

This is what it means to organize chaos—not with perfection, but with presence.

Not with control, but with care.

Not as the loudest voice, but as the clearest one.

▶   *Related Toolkit: Coordination Sheet (Appendix E)*

Daily Anchor for Leading Anyway

I do not fear the mess. Chaos is simply unorganized opportunity. I bring order by calming my mind, clarifying my priorities, and guiding others toward steady ground. My leadership creates rhythm where there was once disorder. I am equipped to bring structure to complexity.

> *Quietly or aloud, say after me:*
> **"I bring order to complexity. I see the pieces clearly. I lead through chaos with calm authority."**

CHAPTER 6 LEADERSHIP SNAPSHOT

 FRAMEWORK IN ACTION

This chapter directly supports three core pillars of the *Global Leadership Framework*:

Operational Clarity: By establishing coordination as a core leadership responsibility—not just logistics.

Adaptive Leadership: By reinforcing the importance of structure without rigidity.

Collective Power and Voice: By inviting others into synchronized effort and distributed leadership roles.

 KEY LEADERSHIP TAKEAWAYS

- Movement without coordination creates burnout, confusion, and duplicated effort.
- Coordination is not about controlling people—it's about channeling energy.
- Leaders must act as anchors and compasses during chaos.
- Structure does not stifle creativity—it unlocks shared momentum.
- Effective coordination makes space for others to lead and contribute.

REFLECTIVE JOURNAL QUESTIONS

1 When urgency strikes, do I default to doing or to directing?

2 How can I organize others without dominating them?

3 What systems or cues help teams regain rhythm in disorder?

CULTURAL INSIGHT

Globally, many crisis responses are sustained not by formal leadership but by shared responsibility. In places like Haiti, Kerala, or the Eastern Cape, coordination often flows through spiritual leaders, local organizers, or kinship structures. Chapter 6 honors this by demonstrating that true leadership involves mapping the invisible lines of trust, culture, and capacity—especially when systems falter.

USE THIS SECTION TO:

- Train school administrators, shelter leads, or NGO teams in rapid coordination
- Help field managers create just-in-time roles for volunteers
- Reinforce team rhythm in emotionally charged environments
- Highlight the difference between action and sustainable alignment

Part III

Culture, Context, and Care

Disaster never strikes a blank slate. It arrives in places already shaped by history, identity, and memory. The ground may shift—but the deeper fractures, formed by injustice, inequality, and generational pain, were there long before the crisis began.

No two communities are alike. Yet too often, crisis response treats them as if they are. When aid arrives without context, and leadership overlooks local dynamics, harm can result—even when intentions are good. What was meant as help can feel like intrusion. What was meant as order can feel like control.

This section reminds us that leadership in times of disaster must be both culturally aware and emotionally attuned. Your tone, pace, posture, and even your presence carry meaning. In many parts of the world, leadership is earned through humility, not hierarchy. Trust is not given to the loudest voice—but to the most respectful one. It is built slowly through shared language, rituals, memory, and emotional consistency. What works in one context may feel rushed, foreign, or even offensive in another.

These chapters guide you to lead with respect—not from a script, but from a place of awareness. You will learn how to lead across generational lines, collaborate with outside institutions without sacrificing local agency, and create emotional safety for communities who have been historically overlooked or harmed. You will be challenged to see through cultural perspectives not your own—and to listen with a heart wide enough to hold both pain and resilience.

Because you are not simply responding to an event—you are stepping into a living narrative. And your leadership will be remembered not for how quickly you acted, but for how deeply you listened, how gently you moved, and how bravely you created space for others to reclaim their voices in the aftermath.

This is the essence of culturally responsive care: leadership that does not arrive with all the answers—but begins with the humility to ask better questions.

Chapter 7

When the System Isn't Ready

Culture, History, and the Realities of Recovery

Disasters do not strike blank slates. They hit communities already shaped by history, hierarchy, and identity. While they expose the cracks in physical systems, they more profoundly reveal fractures in trust, equity, and belonging. These moments illuminate who has historically been acknowledged and who has not.

Disaster recovery efforts often magnify longstanding social divides. In some communities, aid is distributed unevenly—not due to intention, but because of inherited systems that prioritize visibility over vulnerability. Those who are undocumented, linguistically isolated, socially marginalized, or politically silenced may find themselves pushed to the edges of recovery efforts, once again reminded that their pain is not prioritized. When responders arrive unaware of these dynamics, they risk reinforcing the very inequalities that the crisis has exposed.

That is why culturally intelligent leadership is not optional; it is essential. Leaders must ask, who has been left out of past recovery conversations? Whose grief has been silenced? Whose resilience has gone unrecognized?

> "You're not just showing up as an individual. You are arriving as a symbol of systems."

These are not abstract reflections; they are guiding questions that shape how resources are allocated, how trust is built, and how healing begins. Disaster does not reset a community; it reveals it. Leaders who understand this truth are better positioned to rebuild not only systems but also relationships.

You Are Entering a Web of Lived Experience

When you arrive to lead in the wake of a crisis, you are not entering a neutral space. You are stepping into a web of lived experience—stories of resilience, trauma, tradition, and often, injustice. Leadership in this context is not only about decisiveness; it's also about discernment. It involves recognizing who is consistently overlooked, whose pain is minimized, and whose voice has been excluded from recovery conversations time and again.

To lead effectively in these spaces, you must honor the emotional landscape as much as the logistical one. This means understanding that visible wounds are often only part of the picture. Beneath the surface, people carry loss, history, and unspoken truths. Your ability to lead is directly tied to your willingness to notice what remains unsaid—to read the emotional landscape, not just the formal procedures. You are not merely entering a recovery zone; you are stepping into the aftermath of someone's lived experience.

> "Cultural competence is not a credential—it is a commitment."

Cultural Competence as a Daily Practice

Cultural competence is not a credential; it is a daily commitment. It cannot be acquired through checklists, certifications, or one-time training sessions. Instead, it develops through ongoing humility, emotional attunement, and the discipline to listen before acting. True cultural awareness requires the willingness to slow down when urgency demands speed, to observe before intervening, and to remain teachable in environments where your expertise may not be the highest form of wisdom in the room.

This practice is not always comfortable. It may challenge your assumptions, require you to acknowledge what you do not know, and invite you to follow the lead of those most affected. Yet, it is through this discomfort that leadership matures. The leaders who build trust across cultures are those who lead with curiosity, not certainty—those who understand that respect is not something given, but earned moment by moment through behavior, presence, and sincere connection.

Case Example
Trust and Suspicion in South Africa

In a township outside Cape Town, a post-flood aid delivery was delayed because the NGO coordinator—new to the area—insisted on distributing supplies at a local school without consulting the elders. The community initially rejected the effort. However, when the NGO paused, listened, and engaged with respected grandmothers and youth leaders, trust was restored. Delivery resumed the next day—this time, with full community involvement.

Case Example
Economic Collapse in Argentina

In a suburb of Buenos Aires, a public school principal faced dwindling local funding and the potential closure of school meal programs. Amid student panic and staff resignations, she stabilized the school by converting the auditorium into a food pantry and collaborating with churches and retired educators. Although her leadership was not perfect, her emotional grounding transformed chaos into community action.

Case Example
Spain – The Long Shadow of the
Madrid Train Bombings

In March 2004, Madrid was shaken by coordinated bombings on four commuter trains, killing 193 people and injuring nearly 2,000. While emergency services acted swiftly and the nation declared three days of mourning, the emotional aftermath lingered far longer. Families, many of whom were immigrants from North Africa, Latin America, and Eastern Europe, not only faced loss but also struggled with belonging. The grief was not only for lives lost but for identities questioned.

In the years that followed, community-based mental health initiatives and memorial spaces emerged—not from centralized directives, but through teachers, neighbors, and local organizations. A quiet cultural shift began in how Spain approached trauma recovery. Instead of treating survivors solely as victims, educators and social workers encouraged storytelling, art, and intercultural dialogue. One Madrid school invited students of all backgrounds to create a mural honoring those lost, integrating prayers, poems, and colors from across the cultures affected. In this act, grief became shared—and healing became collective.

This story serves as a reminder that recovery involves more than just infrastructure or justice. It encompasses the reclamation of dignity in the wake of destruction. For multicultural communities across Europe and beyond, it presents a model for identity healing that transcends language, borders, and politics.

History Speaks Louder Than Logistics

Across the globe, context matters. In one Kenyan village, the arrival of an outsider might be met with deference. In a South African township, it might be met with suspicion. In Haiti, skepticism toward foreign aid can be shaped by centuries of external control. In the Philippines, trust may depend on shared spiritual values. These reactions are not personal—they are historical. You are not simply showing up as an individual; you are arriving as a symbol of systems that may have helped, harmed, or both.

Ethics of Presence: You Are a Guest, Not a Hero

In communities that carry the memory of colonization, displacement, or institutional neglect, leadership is not granted—it is earned through presence, posture, and restraint. As humanitarian strategist Hugo Slim describes, this requires "the ethics of presence"—the ability to be fully engaged without eclipsing local agency. You are not the hero; you are a guest. Your role is not to rescue but to walk alongside with steadiness, sensitivity, and shared purpose.

Caution: Efficiency Is Not Always Welcome

Well-intentioned missteps often arise from a single false assumption: that your way is the better way. The quickest solution is not always the most welcomed one. A process that feels efficient in Texas may be deeply mistrusted in rural India. A conflict resolution style from Western Europe may fail in areas where indirect communication signifies emotional intelligence. Eye contact, tone of voice, posture, and gender roles—all of these carry different meanings across regions, generations, and belief systems.

Ask Before Acting: Key Questions for Culturally Attuned Leaders

That's why listening is not a delay. It is the leadership. Before offering aid, ask:

- Who has trust in this community?
- Whose guidance do people seek—elders, faith leaders, youth advocates, women's cooperatives?
- Who could be unintentionally excluded by the method I'm proposing?

- Is there a language barrier, an access issue, or a historical injustice that must be acknowledged before it can be healed?

Community Intelligence Is a Core Asset

Community intelligence is one of your most valuable and irreplaceable assets. It resides in relationships, not spreadsheets; in trust, not transactions. It is earned through presence and consistency, not obtained through data collection. Without respect, it remains inaccessible. When honored, it becomes the foundation for solutions that are both effective and culturally rooted.

Case Example
Field Adjustment in the Philippines

In Bohol, Philippines, after a major earthquake, a foreign relief team attempted to implement a medical triage protocol. However, local elders refused to leave the site of the chapel, citing spiritual obligations. Rather than forcing them to relocate, the team adapted by bringing supplies to the site and inviting a local deacon to assist. This approach deepened trust and allowed aid to reach more people.

Layers Within a Nation: America Is Not One Story

Even within a single nation, there are complex cultural realities. A drought in northern Ghana affects pastoral communities differently than it impacts urban residents in Accra. A flood in the United States may simultaneously impact Black communities in Louisiana, undocumented farmworkers in California, and Native elders in South Dakota—each facing distinct needs, histories, and relationships with government support.

This matters because effective disaster response is not just about logistics; it's about legitimacy. If a community does not trust the messenger, they will not trust the message. Black communities that have faced centuries of systemic neglect may view federal aid with suspicion, recalling instances of delayed or denied assistance during past crises. Indigenous communities may carry intergenerational memories of broken treaties and unfulfilled promises, making collaboration with outside agencies emotionally charged. Undocumented workers may hesitate to seek shelter or food out of fear of exposure, even as their homes are being destroyed. These responses are not irrational; they are informed by lived experience.

When leaders fail to recognize these layers, they risk applying a one-size-fits-all solution to a deeply nuanced reality. However, when they approach with humility, cultural awareness, and a willingness to co-lead with local voices, they can transform fear into trust and disruption into restoration. A nation is never just one story. Within each zip code, each shelter, and each relief line, multiple truths unfold simultaneously. The role of a leader is not to simplify those truths but to honor them—so recovery becomes not only possible but also just.

Dignity in Refusal: Cultural Humility in Action

Cultural humility involves examining your own assumptions. When someone declines your help, it may not signify rejection—it may represent dignity. When a mother hesitates to evacuate, it may not indicate ignorance—it may reflect ancestral memory. Perhaps the last time her people left, they were never allowed to return.

In moments like these, effective leadership requires restraint and reverence. It means resisting the urge to override a choice you do not yet understand. It means holding space for lived history, even when it challenges your timeline or task list. Refusal is not always resistance; sometimes it is a form of self-preservation rooted in

"You do not need to erase yourself to be effective. But you do need to lead in a way others recognize as care—not control."

experience. True humility invites us to pause, inquire with care, and let go of the need to be seen as the rescuer. When we honor the meaning behind a "no," we preserve dignity—and we lead with humanity.

What Am I Missing?

To lead across cultures is to remain curious and cautious at the same time. It means asking yourself, "What am I missing?" before assuming expertise. It means noticing how your own background shapes what feels urgent, logical, or respectful. It means knowing when to step up—and when to step back.

This question—simple but powerful—keeps your leadership grounded in humility. "What am I missing?" invites you to consider histories you do not carry, beliefs you do not share, and traumas you may never fully understand. It slows reactive instincts and creates space for deeper observation. You may notice that what feels efficient to you seems disrespectful to others. You may learn that silence in one culture signifies wisdom, not disengagement. Leadership across cultures is not about having all the answers; it is about cultivating enough awareness to recognize when your lens is too narrow. Staying open to what you might be missing is not a sign of weakness. It is the discipline of wise leadership.

Your Logo Carries Weight.

If you come from an NGO, a government agency, or a faith-based organization, remember: your logo carries weight. It can symbolize hope—or betrayal. Culturally informed leadership encompasses emotional literacy. It involves remaining attuned to how others interpret your presence and having the strength to adapt without defensiveness.

In some communities, your arrival may symbolize long-awaited support. In others, it may reopen wounds linked to broken promises, failed interventions, or uneven power dynamics. The emblem on your shirt might evoke comfort—or suspicion—depending on the legacy of those who came before you. This does not mean walking on egg-shells; it means walking with awareness. A culturally competent leader does not assume goodwill—they earn trust through every word, gesture, and decision. Knowing the history behind your organization's reputation in a specific area is not optional—it is essential. Because in crisis settings, perception is not a side note. It is the beginning of every interaction you will have.

2011 Snapshot: The Tsunami's Quiet Leaders (Japan, Tōhoku)

In March 2011, Japan faced one of the most devastating natural disasters in its modern history—a magnitude 9.0 earthquake that triggered a massive tsunami along the Tōhoku coastline. Entire towns were swallowed within minutes. While rescue teams mobilized, it was often teachers, school principals, and community elders who emerged as immediate leaders. In many coastal schools, teachers calmly led evacuation drills they had practiced countless times before, guiding children uphill to safety with steady voices, even as sirens wailed.

In some villages, elderly residents guided younger neighbors to higher ground, drawing from ancestral memories of past tsunamis. Their leadership was characterized not by panic, but by quiet precision, deep trust in preparation, and a collective responsibility for the most vulnerable. Long after the waters receded, these unsung leaders remained present, helping children process grief, supporting displaced families, and guiding emotional recovery alongside physical rebuilding.

Closing Insight: Honor What's Already There

Crisis leadership is not only measured by what you create—it is revealed in how you arrive, how you listen, and how you honor those who have been living the reality long before your presence. Your authority will not be granted by your credentials alone; it will emerge from your ability to respect the knowledge, strength, and resilience already present within the community.

Slow down when necessary. Inquire before making assumptions. Allow space for traditions, languages, and rhythms that are not your own. Leadership that honors culture does more than provide assistance—it rebuilds trust. And trust is the foundation of any sustainable recovery.

You don't need to erase yourself to be effective. However, you do need to lead in a way that others recognize as care—not control.

That is how you assist systems in healing—starting from the inside out.

You were not called to dominate the moment.

You were called to honor it—and to lead it together.

▶   *Related Toolkit: Cultural Checklists for Global Use (Appendix C)*

Daily Anchor for Leading Anyway

Systems may fail, but my leadership does not have to falter with them. I let go of my frustration over what others have not prepared, and I concentrate on what I can create within the moment I am given. I become the stability that others need, even when the system lags behind. My leadership fills the gaps with wisdom, flexibility, and compassion.

> *Quietly or aloud, say after me:*
> **"I rise even when the system stumbles. My leadership adapts, steadies, and carries forward."**

🌐 CHAPTER 7 LEADERSHIP SNAPSHOT 🌐

 FRAMEWORK IN ACTION

This chapter embodies three powerful components of the *Global Leadership Framework*:

Collective Power and Voice: By redefining leadership as action, not authority.

Emotional Centering: By empowering individuals to lead from presence and conviction, even without formal roles.

Cultural Coordination: By affirming that leadership can—and does—emerge organically across all cultures.

 KEY LEADERSHIP TAKEAWAYS

- Disasters don't wait for job titles—leadership begins with willingness.
- Emergent leadership saves lives, especially in under-resourced communities.
- The most impactful leaders are often those who rise without being asked.
- Leadership can sound like a calm voice, not a command.
- Courageous presence often outweighs formal training in moments of crisis.

REFLECTIVE JOURNAL QUESTIONS

1 What has kept me from stepping forward in past moments of need?

2 How can I prepare myself emotionally to lead without being invited?

3 Where in my community do I already see emergent leadership at work?

CULTURAL INSIGHT

Across the globe—from remote villages to urban neighborhoods—emergent leadership serves as the heartbeat of resilience. Whether it's a youth directing traffic in Kenya or a grandmother organizing relief in the Philippines, this form of leadership respects local wisdom, spiritual authority, and community trust. Chapter 7 reminds us that we all have the capacity to transform chaos into care, even without a formal mandate.

USE THIS SECTION TO:

- Empower community members or volunteers who feel unsure of their value
- Train youth leaders, laypersons, or frontline staff to trust their instincts
- Highlight case studies of culturally specific emergent leadership
- Shift your team's mindset from rank to responsibility

Chapter 8

Age-Specific Care

The Emotional Anchor of Generations

Disaster does not merely collapse buildings—it disrupts emotional anchors. For children, that anchor may be the rhythm of school or the steady voice of a caregiver. For elders, it might be a morning ritual, a familiar place of worship, or the simple repetition of daily routines. When those anchors vanish, the result is not just logistical disruption but emotional disorientation. In these moments, leadership must shift from operational to profoundly human.

"Trauma doesn't sound the same in every voice."

Restoring a sense of emotional anchoring is not about returning to normal—it is about creating new moments of stability within the unknown. A familiar song played during a meal distribution in Manila. A gathering of elders in a circle under a tent in Dominica. A youth volunteer reading stories aloud in a shelter in Morocco. These small acts restore continuity, memory, and belonging. They remind people—especially the most vulnerable—that life is still in motion, even during the pause.

For intergenerational communities, leaders must recognize that emotional anchors differ across age groups. Teenagers may crave connection and purpose; young children need safe, predictable rhythms;

older adults seek continuity and legacy. When leaders design their responses with these emotional needs in mind, they foster healing across generations—not just survival.

Leadership in these moments requires listening beyond logistics. It asks: *What brings this person a sense of place? Of identity? Of rhythm?* And how can we quietly return that to them—even in small, imperfect ways? Because when people are emotionally anchored, they start to reorient themselves. From there, they can begin again.

Understanding Emotional Needs Across Ages

Leading across generations is not just about distributing aid; it requires emotional sensitivity to how different age groups experience fear, loss, and uncertainty. Trauma does not sound the same in every voice. It manifests in a five-year-old differently than in a seventy-five-year-old. What soothes one may unsettle another, and what empowers one may overwhelm another. Yet, all are searching for a steadying presence amid the chaos.

Children often express distress through behavior—restlessness, silence, or clinging to adults. They may not fully understand the situation, but they sense the emotional tone around them. Their ability to regulate emotions depends on us. Elders, on the other hand, may internalize their fear or express it as frustration or stoicism. They often carry not only the present loss but also echoes of past disruptions—wars, migrations, previous disasters—that shape their responses.

Adolescents may appear disengaged, but their silence often conceals overwhelm. They are in a developmental phase where independence matters—and losing autonomy during a crisis can feel particularly disorienting. Adults in the middle, often caregivers themselves, may suppress their own emotions to maintain stability for others, resulting in an emotional backlog that surfaces later.

Understanding these generational differences enables leaders to respond with nuance. A quiet room for elders, a play space for children, meaningful tasks for teens, and peer spaces for adults can create emotional balance amid external chaos. It is not about providing the same support to everyone—it is about honoring what support means to different people.

When leadership addresses age-specific emotional needs, it becomes not only more compassionate but also more effective. In this way, emotional intelligence is not merely an add-on to disaster response; it is an essential skill for helping people of all ages find stability in the storm.

Children: Safety Through Steadiness

Children often don't articulate distress—they express it. Some go silent. Others act out. Some revert to behaviors they had previously outgrown—bedwetting, thumb-sucking, separation anxiety. These are not behavioral issues; they are nervous system responses to unpredictable change. Children seek safety not through words but through tone, routine, and proximity.

You don't need perfect language; you need presence. A calm voice, consistent actions, and gentle boundaries are essential. A simple phrase like "You're safe now," spoken with sincerity, can begin to re-anchor their sense of security. Five minutes of undivided attention from a calm adult can create a profound moment of re-regulation. Even temporary routines—structured play, storytelling, and drawing spaces—provide children a sense of control when everything else feels unstable.

Case Example
Post-Fire School Circle in Australia

In Victoria, Australia, after a bushfire swept through a rural community, a teacher quietly established a simple yet powerful daily practice. Each morning, she gathered her students in a circle and encouraged them to share one thing they missed the most—a pet, a favorite tree, a lost toy, or the comfort of home. This small act of naming their grief allowed the children to express their losses without feeling overwhelmed. Over time, the circle evolved from a routine into a shared space of healing and safety. Both staff and students found steadiness in this ritual, which honored what had been lost while gently rebuilding connections, trust, and a sense of emotional belonging amid ongoing recovery.

Elders: Honor, Not Just Help

Just as children are uniquely vulnerable, so are elders. They may face greater physical risks during a disaster, but their emotional invisibility afterward can be just as dangerous. Many carry the weight of prior displacement, generational trauma, or unresolved grief. Some lose access to essential medicines, assistive devices, or familiar caregivers. Others feel overwhelmed by noise, confusion, or rapid changes in their environment.

In some cultures, elders are revered and consulted, while in others, they are quietly set aside. Regardless of the context, elders need to feel included—not managed, patronized, or ignored. Ask for their perspective and invite their wisdom. When memory, mobility, or communication become barriers, slow down. Speak gently, create quiet zones, and let them move at their own pace—even if urgency surrounds you.

Multigenerational Families: Layered Support Systems

Many families juggle multiple roles at once—raising children while also caring for aging parents. In these households, pressure builds quickly. Parents and caregivers often set aside their own needs to look after both ends of the generational spectrum. Leadership in this context involves more than responding to immediate needs. It entails designing relief efforts that safeguard emotional sustainability.

> "Children don't seek safety through words—they seek it through tone, routine, and proximity."

Provide child-friendly spaces, even in temporary shelters. Create shaded rest areas or separate seating zones for older adults. Assign a calm, consistent voice to explain processes in familiar terms. These small actions carry more weight than you might think. They convey respect, care, and structure—especially when routines have been disrupted.

Community-Based Wisdom: Protect What's Already Working

Around the world, care systems often emerge organically. A grandmother becomes a safe haven for neighborhood children. Teenagers take on protective roles for younger siblings. Local elders gather the names of those who are missing. These acts are not makeshift—they are cultural intelligence in motion. Do not override them with imported models. Support them. Resource them. Learn from them.

Case Example
Informal Check-In System in India

In Tamil Nadu, India, following cyclone damage, a retired headmistress established a chalkboard in her neighborhood to provide daily community updates. Local children took turns writing messages for elders who couldn't walk to the town center. This intergenerational coordination became the heart of community connection for weeks.

Trusting the Signs of Emotional Overwhelm

In areas such as West Africa, Southeast Asia, and Indigenous communities across the Americas, caregiving is not viewed as an individual burden—it is a shared cultural rhythm, a strength interwoven into daily life. These collective systems have long supported communities through hardship. Yet even the most resilient traditions can be stressed by the weight of prolonged trauma.

Emotional overwhelm does not always announce itself in obvious ways. A once-curious child may become quiet. An elder who once led songs may stop attending gatherings. A once-unshakable community volunteer may start missing shifts. These are not signs of weakness—they are messages. They are signals that the emotional current beneath the surface is rising faster than the system can absorb.

Leadership in these moments is not about enforcing normalcy; it is about honoring disruption. It means recognizing these behavioral shifts as sacred clues rather than problems to be fixed. Your role is not to silence the discomfort but to make room for it—allowing space for tears, pauses, absences, and heaviness.

To lead with compassion is to listen for what remains unsaid. In communities where silence carries weight, where gestures speak louder than words, and where dignity must be maintained even in sorrow, leadership must slow down enough to notice the subtle cues. Not to control them—but to respect them. Because the road to healing does not start with answers. It begins with acknowledgment.

Recovery Without the Rush

Recovery is not about pushing people to recover and rebuild quickly after disruption; it is about allowing space for healing, adaptation, and steady progress. It's about giving them the room to feel, adapt, and reconnect at their own pace. Allow children to be noisy, curious, and uncertain without punishment. Let elders maintain their quiet presence. Let caregivers breathe. And let healing resemble a shared rhythm slowly returning—not a forced march toward normalcy.

The Teacher With Shaking Hands

The announcement came over the intercom without warning. "Lockdown. This is not a drill."

The teacher's heart instantly started to race. She had practiced the procedures before, training for scenarios she hoped would never occur. Now, in real time, she moved quickly — securing the door, turning off the lights, directing her students to the corner of the room where they would be least visible.

The children looked up at her, wide-eyed and silent. Some clutched their backpacks, while one began to cry softly, trying to muffle the sound. She crouched beside them, whispering reassurances that she could barely believe herself.

Her hands trembled as she texted the administrator to confirm that her classroom was secure. She could feel adrenaline rushing through her veins, but she fought to keep her voice steady. The students were watching. The staff was watching. In that moment, she understood the weight of being the calm in the room.

The lockdown lasted just thirty minutes. The threat turned out to be a false alarm. However, the impact of those minutes would remain with her long after.

Leadership in a crisis does not always feel heroic. Often, it feels like trying to steady your own heartbeat while others rely on you to steady theirs.

2015 Snapshot: The Work of Belonging (Sweden, Refugee Integration)

Beginning in 2015, Sweden became one of the major destinations for refugees fleeing conflict in Syria, Afghanistan, and other war-torn areas. While national policies allowed entry, the true leadership challenge arose within local communities. Teachers welcomed children into trauma-sensitive classrooms, establishing language bridges while easing fears rooted in displacement. Social workers acted as cultural guides, assisting families in navigating new systems of healthcare, housing, and employment.

Municipal councils organized neighborhood dialogue circles to build trust between newcomers and long-established residents. Faith leaders opened sanctuaries for counseling, prayer, and quiet refuge. In these towns and cities, leadership meant much more than enforcing policy—it required emotional patience, cultural humility, and the slow, continuous effort of fostering belonging one conversation at a time. These local leaders did not merely provide services; they created the emotional scaffolding that enabled displaced families to gradually rebuild their sense of home.

Closing Insight: Leading With Compassion Across Ages

Leadership in age-specific care is not just a task—it's a ministry. It is the quiet reweaving of connections across generations. It is presence without pressure, clarity without condescension, and compassion that honors every stage of life with equal dignity.

Disaster recovery involves more than just rebuilding structures; it also means restoring the invisible bonds that unite communities. It recognizes that an elder's story holds equal urgency to a child's cry, that a caregiver's exhaustion is just as deserving of care as a patient's wound, and that every voice—regardless of age or experience—merits being heard.

> "Leadership in age-specific care is not a task—it's a ministry."

When we keep that in mind, we do more than recover — we help every generation feel seen, safe, and significant once again. We build emotional foundations alongside physical ones. We create space for memory, for hope, and for healing to flow through the community — not as an afterthought, but as a guiding force.

In doing so, we affirm that true leadership is not defined by the number of people we command, but by the compassion we extend across every age, every moment, and every fragile heartbeat that dares to believe in what comes next.

▶ *Related Toolkit: Age-Specific Support Quick Guide (Appendix D)*

Daily Anchor for Leading Anyway

Every person I serve carries unique needs, shaped by age, stage, and experience. I meet each individual where they are, adjusting my approach with care, wisdom, and emotional understanding. My leadership honors both the child and the elder, the dependent and the caregiver. I lead with sensitivity, not assumption.

> *Quietly or aloud, say after me:*
> **"I lead with discernment. I see the person in front of me and respond with wisdom and care."**

🌐 CHAPTER 8 LEADERSHIP SNAPSHOT 🌐

 FRAMEWORK IN ACTION

This chapter advances three core elements of the *Global Leadership Framework*:

Cultural Coordination: By encouraging sensitivity to developmental needs and generational norms.

Operational Clarity: By emphasizing the need for age-appropriate structures, spaces, and supports.

Emotional Centering: By recognizing that different age groups express distress—and healing—in different ways.

 KEY LEADERSHIP TAKEAWAYS

▷ Children and elders experience and express crisis differently—and require different care.

▷ Routines, grounding rituals, and safe spaces are critical for children in upheaval.

▷ Elders may hold community memory and spiritual insight—honoring them strengthens collective resilience.

▷ Emotional literacy must be age-adjusted, not one-size-fits-all.

▷ The way you speak, assign roles, and design support must reflect developmental awareness.

REFLECTIVE JOURNAL QUESTIONS

1 How do I currently adapt my leadership approach for different age groups?

2 What assumptions might I hold about the emotional resilience of children or elders?

3 Where can I improve inclusivity across generational needs in my crisis response?

CULTURAL INSIGHT

In many cultures, elders are revered as wisdom carriers and children as sacred continuity. During disaster recovery, overlooking either group disrupts not only care—but identity. Chapter 8 reinforces the global norm of intergenerational respect, reminding leaders that how we treat our most vulnerable shapes our collective healing.

USE THIS SECTION TO:

- Train shelter managers, teachers, and volunteers in age-sensitive crisis practices
- Structure debriefs and interventions by age group
- Design youth-specific safe zones and elder-inclusive recovery roles
- Encourage culturally responsive care that honors generational dignity

Chapter 9

Coordinating with Outside Help

The Challenge of Collaboration

Disasters may begin locally, but the response rarely remains that way. Aid comes from beyond the community—nonprofits, NGOs, international volunteers, government agencies, and faith-based relief teams. These groups provide critical resources and expertise, but they also introduce complexity: cultural mismatches, layered power dynamics, and, at times, unintentional harm.

> "Presence comes before programs."

What begins as help can quickly shift into hierarchy. Outside actors may arrive with urgency, technology, and funding—but without a deep understanding of local relationships, customs, or leadership norms. Communities that have long navigated crises on their own terms may suddenly feel overrun or silenced in the name of efficiency. And when language barriers, unacknowledged trauma histories, or colonial legacies remain unaddressed, tension can quietly build beneath the surface of even well-meaning partnerships.

True collaboration during disaster response requires more than coordination; it demands humility. It necessitates that external teams recognize they are entering a story mid-chapter—not to lead it, but to support it. It also challenges local leaders to make space for outside help without losing sight of their community's needs and voice.

Successful collaboration is not about who leads but rather about how leadership is shared. It involves creating space for mutual learning, respecting lived experiences alongside professional expertise, and building trust in real-time. In the best cases, it focuses on transformation—not just recovery—as diverse teams model a new way of moving forward together.

The Role of the Local Leader

As a local leader, you often find yourself positioned between two worlds: the community you live in and the institutions that come to help. You translate urgent needs into funding proposals, interpret local values for external actors, and absorb the emotional tension when systems designed to assist start to feel overwhelming.

This position is demanding—but essential. Because no matter how well-meaning the support, it is rarely as informed as it believes. Outsiders may bring funding, staff, or supplies, but you provide something more vital: lived context, cultural memory, and relational trust.

Presence Before Programs

Coordination begins not with logistics but with presence. Not all assistance feels helpful. A global NGO may arrive with systems that overlook cultural rhythms. A donor may prioritize photo opportunities over actual needs. A foreign government may send aid without fully understanding the terrain. If left unchecked, the community becomes a target of intervention rather than a partner in recovery.

> "Some organizations understand inventory—but not grief. Logistics—but not dignity."

Your leadership disrupts this pattern. You're not just a messenger; you're the cultural interpreter, the emotional compass, and the advocate for community agency. That means speaking up when something doesn't fit. Saying, clearly and without apology: "That won't work here," or "Here's what we need first."

Discernment, Not Defiance

In urgent settings, where resources are limited and tensions run high, leadership often becomes a test of emotional clarity. It can be tempting to either embrace every offer of help without question—or reject outside assistance altogether out of fear of losing control or cultural integrity. However, sustainable leadership does not operate from extremes. It exists in the tension. It poses hard questions. It listens before reacting.

Discernment is not hesitation—it is wisdom in action. It means taking a moment to evaluate, not from ego, but from care. The work of coordination is not a checklist—it is a living, dynamic relationship with the needs of the moment and the identity of the community.

That discernment may sound like:

- *What do we need most right now—not in theory, but in reality?*
- *Who is best equipped to offer that—not just based on title, but based on trust?*
- *What must we protect, even if the resource looks attractive on the surface?*

You may find that some organizations arrive prepared—with systems, funding, and structure. However, they may lack soul. They understand inventory but not grief. They track logistics but overlook stories. They deliver supplies but forget to see the people.

That's where you come in.

You are not just a middle person. You are the emotional interpreter of the moment. You carry the memory of the community—the rhythms, the relationships, and the rituals that can't be found in any spreadsheet. Your role is not to say yes to everything. It is to protect the integrity of what matters most, even when others do not fully grasp it.

This type of leadership may be subtle. It may go unnoticed by external partners. However, it is the kind of leadership that ensures recovery does not erase culture, that aid does not replace agency, and that service does not turn into saviorism.

Discernment is your act of dignity. It transforms coordination into care and will help your community not just survive the crisis, but emerge with its heart intact.

Case Example
Partnership Pitfalls in Haiti

After the 2010 earthquake, international agencies in Haiti established camps and aid distribution sites while often excluding local leaders from the planning process. In one Port-au-Prince district, residents eventually organized their own food distribution after outsiders misjudged community needs. Their local structure outlasted the temporary support, reminding everyone involved that resilience must be rooted locally.

Case Example
Lebanon Economic Crisis & Blast Recovery

Following the Beirut port explosion in 2020, Lebanon's severely strained government institutions struggled to coordinate large-scale recovery efforts. In the absence of a coordinated state response, local nonprofit organizations, churches, and neighborhood councils led the initial efforts—clearing debris, distributing meals, repairing homes, and providing emotional support. However, as international aid poured in, tensions arose when foreign agencies attempted to centralize control without fully understanding Lebanon's complex political and sectarian landscape. It was the local leaders' quiet negotiation skills that ultimately brokered partnerships and preserved community dignity amid global attention.

Advocacy Without Apology

You may need to confront organizations that prioritize speed over sensitivity. You may need to pause initiatives that lack consent or cultural alignment. When donors value visibility more than outcomes, you may need to protect the community from becoming a mere campaign. When funding comes with restrictions that silence local voices, you may need to walk away. And when you do, it will be hard. But it's necessary.

In places such as the Philippines, local barangay captains frequently act as informal negotiators between aid organizations and the community. In rural India, self-help groups and women's collectives often mobilize more quickly than formal agencies.

Case Example
Faith-Based Response in Hawaii

During the 2023 wildfires in Maui, community churches opened their doors to evacuees before federal aid arrived. One church leader organized medical support from local nurses and coordinated with donors from other islands. By the time national organizations arrived, the system was already in place. Instead of disrupting it, those who listened improved it.

Let history remind us: local leadership is not secondary. It is central.

Case Example
Earthquake Response in Turkey

Following the 2023 earthquakes in Turkey, many village elders in rural Hatay province took the lead when international organizations arrived. While global teams brought heavy equipment, local elders organized food sharing, coordinated prayer spaces, and upheld cultural mourning traditions that calmed anxious families. External responders who took time to engage with elders first were granted greater community trust, while those who pushed for quick control often faced resistance. Partnership was most effective when outside expertise proceeded at the pace of community wisdom.

Partnership with Boundaries

Despite the complications, not all outside help is misaligned. Some NGOs truly listen. Some donors are willing to learn. Some institutions are open to collaboration. These are moments of opportunity—but they require clarity and courage from you.

Set expectations early. Ask for inclusion in planning. Advocate for local hiring, fair compensation, and decision-making power. Insist on transparency—especially when promises are made publicly. And whenever possible, slow the process down long enough for relationships to form before implementation begins.

Protecting Emotional Terrain

You are not just coordinating logistics; you are protecting trust. Trust in leaders. Trust in institutions. Trust in one another. When outside help moves on—and it often does—your leadership will remain. That means safeguarding your own credibility is as important as distributing their resources.

> "Model what it looks like to welcome support without surrendering agency."

Model how to welcome support without giving up agency. Invite partnership without fostering dependence. Rebuild not only what was lost, but also the deeper fabric of community life that allows people to belong.

2023 Snapshot: The Fire That Stole a History (Lahaina, Hawaii Wildfire)

In August 2023, the historic town of Lahaina on Maui experienced one of the deadliest wildfires in modern U.S. history. Hurricane-driven winds fueled the flames with terrifying speed, leaving residents with little to no warning. Families jumped into the ocean to escape the intense heat and smoke. Entire cultural landmarks were engulfed within hours. Cell towers collapsed. Power failed. Yet, amid the devastation, neighbors helped neighbors to safety.

Store managers opened warehouses as shelters. Community elders comforted frightened children as the flames approached. Volunteers used personal boats to ferry families to safer ground. In the face of staggering loss, leadership emerged not through formal systems but through ordinary people choosing to act. Long after the smoke cleared, the work of grief, restoration, and cultural preservation continued—carried by those who had witnessed their community's history reduced to ash.

Closing Insight: Leading from Within

You may not have the funding, workforce, or global influence of a large organization. However, you possess something they cannot mimic: proximity. Insight. Endurance. You understand not only what has broken, but also what has always been fragile. You hold the knowledge of where trust resides—and how it can be restored.

When outside help aligns with that knowledge, true recovery becomes possible. Not because someone saved the day, but because someone like you stood firm in the gap—guiding the process with clarity, compassion, and care.

▶ *Related Toolkit: Field Templates (Appendix E)*

Daily Anchor for Leading Anyway

True leadership does not fear collaboration. I recognize that I am not called to carry everything alone. By coordinating with others, I expand the strength of what can be accomplished. My leadership is not diminished by partnership — it is multiplied through shared expertise, trust, and humility.

> *Quietly or aloud, say after me:*
> **"I lead with openness. Collaboration strengthens my leadership. Together, we accomplish more."**

🌐 CHAPTER 9 LEADERSHIP SNAPSHOT 🌐

 FRAMEWORK IN ACTION

This chapter activates three key components of the *Global Leadership Framework*:

Cultural Coordination: By addressing power dynamics between local leaders and external aid groups.

Operational Clarity: By reinforcing clear boundaries, protocols, and trust-building between unfamiliar systems.

Collective Power and Voice: By centering local leadership in conversations with external entities.

KEY LEADERSHIP TAKEAWAYS

- Outside help should enhance—not override—local knowledge and effort.
- Coordination requires respect, not assumption, from both sides.
- Local voices must remain central, even when external resources arrive.
- Clarity in communication and chain of command prevents chaos.
- Emotional intelligence helps mediate trust between unfamiliar partners.

REFLECTIVE JOURNAL QUESTIONS

1. How do I ensure that outside help strengthens rather than displaces local efforts?

2. What boundaries need to be clearly communicated when collaborating with external teams?

3. How do I advocate for local voices without creating tension?

CULTURAL INSIGHT

Around the world, communities often receive "help" that unintentionally replicates colonial patterns—entering with authority, extracting data, or setting up systems without consent. Chapter 9 encourages leaders to insist on partnership over paternalism, ensuring that local culture, memory, and rhythm are preserved.

USE THIS SECTION TO:

- Prepare local teams to coordinate with NGOs, international agencies, or military support
- Train external volunteers in cultural humility and partnership
- Establish shared protocols, debrief structures, and respect practices
- Facilitate smoother collaboration across aid systems and community responders

Part IV

Holding the Emotional Landscape

Long after the crisis ends, the emotions remain—and they need somewhere safe to land.

When the physical work is finished, the emotional work begins. The adrenaline fades. The systems reset. The supplies are counted and distributed. But within people, something lingers—grief that won't be spoken aloud, anger that simmers beneath the surface, and exhaustion that no amount of sleep can alleviate.

This is where many leaders falter. Not because they don't care, but because they were never taught how to bear the weight of what follows.

These chapters provide guidance for navigating the invisible waves that follow the storm. You'll learn to recognize unspoken grief, respond to anger that conceals deeper pain, and care for your own body and mind before burnout sets in. You'll discover how to rebuild trust—not just in systems, but in one another—and how to embody hope in ways that feel sincere, not performative.

This part of the journey requires no cape, no perfect words—only presence and the willingness to sit beside people during the toughest moments of their healing without pushing them toward resolution.

You are not just a leader in a crisis; you are a witness, a stabilizer, and a reminder that emotional recovery is not weakness—it is wisdom.

Chapter 10

Crisis Within the Crisis

The emotional cost of leading while personally unraveling.

GLOBAL REALITY CHECK
NO ONE ESCAPES CRISIS ANYMORE

We are no longer living in a world where disaster feels distant. Crisis is no longer a matter of *if*, but *where* and *when*. The question is not whether it will arrive—but whether we will be ready to respond with presence, clarity, and care when it does.

On May 31, 2025, panic erupted on a packed subway train in Seoul when a man ignited a fire mid-commute, forcing 160 people to flee as smoke surged through the tunnels. Days later, in China's Guizhou Province, floodwaters surged past 13 feet in Rongjiang County, displacing over 80,000 residents and destroying homes that had stood for generations. Across the globe, in Indonesia, a 27-year-old Brazilian woman fell nearly 500 meters near an active volcano while hiking—a tragedy that unfolded over four excruciating days as rescue teams raced against terrain and time. And on the same week, in southern Brazil, a

"Grief after disaster does not always look like mourning."

hot-air balloon caught fire mid-flight, forcing terrified passengers to jump. Eight did not survive.

These are not isolated events. They are snapshots of a global reality where disruption is constant, and emotional resilience is no longer optional—it is the core of sustainable leadership.

Whether you are in Seoul or Shanghai, Brazil or Botswana, cri-sis has become part of the human condition. It will reach into cities and villages, boardrooms and classrooms, homes and transit lines. And each time it does, someone will need to step forward—not with perfection, but with presence. Not with control, but with calm.

Leadership after the storm requires more than logistics. It demands humanity.

Framework in Action

The Global Leadership Framework teaches that when crisis becomes a shared condition—not an isolated event—leaders must shift from reactive responders to emotionally equipped anchors. From Seoul's subway to the floodplains of Guizhou, leaders were needed not just for evacuation, but for presence: to calm voices, hold eye contact, and make humane decisions in compressed time.

Sustainable leadership under global disruption hinges on a readiness that is internal, not just institutional. It requires emotional regulation under pressure, trust-building when systems collapse, and the ability to move from fear to focus without bypassing the human cost. When we train leaders to lead beyond borders and industries, we prepare them for the reality we now live in—where crisis does not ask for credentials, only courage.

Reflective Journal Prompt

When you imagine the next crisis reaching your community, what role are you most prepared to play?

What emotion would you need to manage first in yourself in order to lead others with clarity?

Collective Model Highlight

In the Philippines, *bayanihan*—a cultural principle of collective community action—has long guided disaster response. When floods or typhoons strike, neighbors act without hesitation, moving homes, carrying children, and preparing meals for displaced families. There is no need to be asked. This instinct toward compassionate coordination is a reminder that leadership is often communal—and resilience is strongest when shared.

• • ◦ • •

The Emotional Aftershock

Some storms pass quickly, while others linger—in the silence, sleepless nights, and disruption of routines that no longer feel familiar. Long after the headlines fade and supplies are distributed, a deeper crisis often begins. It is quiet and invisible to outsiders, yet it is everywhere.

> "This isn't a failure of leadership— it's the cost of collective trauma surfacing."

It shows in eyes that evade contact. In children who cease playing. In elders who speak less and gaze more. In arguments that ignite over trivial matters. In trusted team members who suddenly withdraw. It resides in the nervous system, in the altered rhythms of a community, in the stories people stop sharing.

This is the emotional aftershock, and it is just as real—and just as disruptive—as the initial event. It may not make the news, but it shapes every step of recovery. People are not just rebuilding homes—they are relearning how to feel safe in them. They are not just reopening schools—they are navigating grief inside classrooms. They are not just restoring services—they are living with the weight of what was lost.

Leaders who understand this invisible layer of crisis—who pause to acknowledge it, name it, and make room for healing—offer more than just aid. They offer care. They remind people that it's normal to still feel shaken, even when the world seems to have moved on.

To lead through recovery is to become fluent in silence, gestures, and the emotional cues that signal what words cannot. It is to view the human nervous system as part of the infrastructure. It is also to remember that just because something is unspoken does not mean it is unfelt. Emotional aftershocks may be quiet—but they demand a leadership that listens nonetheless.

The Quiet Weight of Grief

Grief after a disaster does not always manifest as mourning. Sometimes it appears as irritability. Occasionally, it expresses itself through blame. Often, it conceals itself behind busyness, emotional shutdown, or silence. In community settings, it frequently ebbs and flows—showing resistance to new plans, unexpected outbursts, or an unexplainable heaviness during group meetings.

If you're leading during this phase, you may feel disoriented. The urgent work seems to be done. Systems are in place. Recovery has begun. But something beneath it all feels more challenging now—emotionally complex and less cooperative. This isn't a failure of leadership; it's the cost of collective trauma finally surfacing.

In many cultures, grief is expressed communally—through mourning rituals, music, shared meals, prayer, and physical acts of remembrance. However, when those practices are disrupted—or when the grief itself becomes too tangled to name—pain can become trapped. Trapped in the body, in the household, and in the silence between people who once connected easily.

People are not just grieving what they lost; they are grieving what will never return: a sense of safety, a familiar rhythm, a favorite tree, a beloved pet, a neighbor who didn't make it, and a way of life now permanently changed.

Case Example
Mourning Together in the Philippines

In Eastern Visayas, Philippines, after Typhoon Haiyan, one village organized a candlelit naming ritual to honor those who were lost. A list of
the deceased was read aloud, with families adding names as the cer-
emony unfolded. No formal therapy was provided; instead, the ritual
itself became a community-wide act of collective mourning. Silence
gave way to sobbing, and then to quiet singing. In that shared space of
loss, the first threads of healing quietly emerged.

Case Example
NHS Crisis Team Leadership in London

During the peak of the COVID-19 pandemic, London hospitals
faced immense pressure as intensive care units reached capacity. While
national guidelines provided protocols, it was often internal crisis
teams—nurse supervisors, department heads, and staff coordinators—
who stabilized day-to-day operations. Senior nurses established rotating rest schedules to preserve mental health, while emotional support
teams conducted check-ins between shifts. In some units, staff organized informal "recovery rooms" where frontline workers could pause,
breathe, and decompress for even a few minutes between overwhelming cases. These micro-leadership adjustments helped sustain teams
through prolonged emotional exhaustion when the system offered
few easy solutions.

Leadership Through the Unspoken

Your role in this season is not to resolve grief. It is to recognize it.
To create space where it can breathe without being rushed, redirected,
or hidden. Grief is not a detour from recovery—it is part of it.

This might mean slowing down meetings to let emotions settle before decisions are made. It might mean allowing for silence instead of filling every pause with urgency. It might mean checking on someone who stopped showing up, not to demand their return, but to remind them they are missed. Sometimes it means being the one to name the collective ache when others avoid it.

In Haiti, after the quake, elders led ceremonies with no words—only their presence. In Japan, following tsunami losses, silent walks became rituals of mourning and solidarity. In refugee camps, songs and prayer circles emerge—not for answers, but for acknowledgment. These unspoken acts become the heartbeat of emotional leadership.

Simply saying, "This is hard. We are not the same. And we are still here," can be more healing than any formal plan. It gives people permission to feel. It tells them that their sorrow does not disqualify them from belonging. And it reminds them that strength is not the absence of emotion—it is the willingness to hold it without looking away.

Leadership through the unspoken is leadership through presence. Not to fix, but to witness. Not to solve, but to steady. It is in these quiet moments that recovery deepens—and that people begin to believe healing is possible.

The Role of Anger in Recovery

Alongside grief comes anger. It can arise quietly or explosively. It may be directed at institutions, absent leaders, or even yourself. However, it's often not personal—it represents a form of grief that has nowhere else to go. People start to confront what could have been prevented, what was withheld, who didn't show up, and why.

This anger, though painful, is not always destructive. When acknowledged and channeled, it becomes part of the collective story—a fuel for advocacy, a push for reform, a cry for dignity.

Do not interpret every sharp word as an attack. Sometimes, you are the only one safe enough to receive it. Leadership in these moments means standing firm while others release the weight they can no longer bear. Hold your center—but remain gentle. Listen. Set boundaries without punishing emotions. And when the moment passes, gently guide the group back toward shared meaning and purpose.

Case Example
Dr. Lorna Breen – Leading Until She Couldn't

In the early days of the COVID-19 pandemic, Dr. Lorna Breen served as the medical director of the emergency department at New York Presbyterian Allen Hospital. Known for her brilliance, compassion, and resilience, she led her team through some of the most devastating weeks of the crisis. The hospital was overwhelmed with patients, resources were strained, and death was a constant presence. Dr. Breen worked tirelessly—day after day—coordinating care, comforting families, supporting staff, and striving to keep everyone moving forward.

Then she contracted the virus herself. After a brief recovery, she returned to work, determined to resume her role. But what was once a calling had become an unbearable burden. The emotional and psychological weight of what she had witnessed—and what she could not fix—continued to grow. She showed up, kept leading, and tried to stay strong. Yet inside, she was unraveling.

In late April 2020, Dr. Breen died by suicide. Her death sent shockwaves through the medical community and served as a sobering reminder of the hidden emotional toll that leadership can exact during a crisis. "She tried to do her job, and it killed her," her father later said.

Her story represents the crisis within a crisis: the moment when the cost of supporting others becomes too great to bear alone. Dr. Breen's leadership was characterized by courage and commitment, but also by isolation, pressure, and a lack of emotional support. Like many leaders, she was expected to be the one others depended on—even as she herself was crumbling.

This example reminds us that emotional collapse is not a failure of character. It often results from systemic neglect, internalized expectations, and a lack of spaces for leaders to process their own pain. Leadership during a disaster must include room for grief, rest, and vulnerability. Otherwise, the weight of responsibility—carried too long and too quietly—can become fatal.

Holding Space—Without Rushing Healing

This is the sacred work of communal holding. It's not about fixing. It's not about controlling. It's about presence. About anchoring someone in the reality that even their most shattered moments do not make them unworthy of care.

To hold space means witnessing without judgment, listening without the need to reply, and remaining present even when silence becomes heavy. It is a radical act of emotional restraint—resisting the urge to rush, solve, or soothe discomfort too quickly. In a world that glorifies speed and resolution, holding space honors process and slowness. It acknowledges the truth that healing is not linear. Pain does not adhere to deadlines. Grief has a rhythm all its own.

When a person is unraveling, they often don't need a leader with all the answers. They need someone steady enough to remain while the questions persist. Someone who can sit in the tension between hope and heartbreak without collapsing into false certainty. Someone who understands that silence can be as sacred as speech—and that tears, shaking hands, or blank stares are not signs of failure, but signs of impact.

Holding space also requires humility—the humility to acknowledge that you cannot carry someone else's pain for them, but you can walk beside them. You can offer your presence as a form of emotional scaffolding—something they can lean against while their inner world slowly rebuilds.

This captures the essence of trauma-informed leadership. It does not demand performance. It does not require perfection. It allows grief to be messy. It creates space for slow breaths, awkward pauses, and unsaid things that may never be fully spoken—but that still deserve to be felt.

Quietly, this kind of leadership tells people: *You're not broken. You're not a burden. And you don't have to do this alone.*

That is how healing begins—not by rushing forward, but by resting safely in the presence of someone who stays.

Case Example
Group Stillness in California

After mass evacuations due to wildfires in Sonoma County, a shelter coordinator initiated "quiet hour" every evening. No announcements. No planning. Just space for people to sit with music, silence, or journaling. The result? A shift in the emotional climate—more tears, yes—but also more peace. It became a daily moment of presence and unspoken support.

And if you are grieving as well, let that be genuine. You are not expected to be unaffected. But you are invited to be honest. To say, "I feel it too. But I'm here." That kind of presence is more powerful than mere composure. It builds trust. It models emotional integrity.

Standing Beside, But Not Inside

The hurricane had passed days ago, but the streets still bore its weight. Waterlogged homes, splintered trees, families gathering what little could be salvaged. I stood with my clipboard in hand—part of the team documenting the damage, processing claims, and helping people take the first administrative steps toward recovery.

As an adjuster, my role was to organize the paperwork and help people move forward. However, standing in front of each family, I often felt the quiet tension that accompanied the work: I was there because of their loss, yet I was not experiencing their loss myself.

A woman guided me through the remnants of her living room, where damp photographs clung to warped floorboards. She explained what was missing, what was ruined, and what the storm had taken. Her voice remained steady, but her eyes revealed the exhaustion beneath it. She was holding it together—for now.

"What cannot be fixed can still be held."

I nodded. I listened. I documented.

Yet, beneath my professionalism, I felt a small, quiet discomfort: the awareness that I could go home that night to dry walls and a full refrigerator. I was helping, but I was not inside her grief. I could witness, but not fully carry.

There is a delicate balance in this kind of work. Too much distance can feel cold. Too much identification risks becoming overwhelming or inauthentic. Real leadership in these moments requires something more nuanced: presence without presumption. Care without performance. The ability to honor someone's pain without needing to mirror it.

Sometimes, the greatest gift you can offer is not a shared experience—it is a steady presence. A voice that is calm. An ear that listens. A face that does not flinch. You do not need to feel what they feel to create emotional safety for what they are carrying.

As the day comes to a close, you hold onto fragments of what you've experienced—not as your own trauma, but as subtle reminders of how delicate and valuable stability truly is.

Leadership in disaster often means standing beside—but not inside— the storm, and doing so with humility, care, and emotional discipline.

2025 Snapshot: The Weight of Prolonged Conflict

Even as new disasters emerged in 2025, older crises deepened around the globe. In Ukraine, Sudan, Gaza, Haiti, and other fragile regions, conflict, displacement, and violence persisted into another year. For local leaders—teachers in war-torn schools, aid workers navigating barricades, faith leaders caring for grief-stricken families—the work remained as burdensome as ever. They led without certainty. Without rest. Without knowing when, or if, relief would arrive. In these places, leadership is not defined by grand speeches but by the quiet endurance of those who continue to manage broken systems while carrying broken hearts.

Closing Insight: What Cannot Be Fixed, Can Still Be Held

Across regions—from coastal towns in the Philippines to mountain villages in Nepal to rural communities in the American South—the grief that follows disaster often lingers in unseen ways. However, in each setting, one truth remains: healing begins in shared presence, not rushed solutions.

Disasters destroy more than just infrastructure. They disturb the soul. Recovering from such profound loss requires more than time; it demands patience, safety, and leadership that accommodates the full range of emotions.

Some things won't return. Some things will never be the same. However, the steady presence of a compassionate leader—one who can name the ache without fear and create emotional safety without fleeing—becomes a source of quiet hope.

Not because the pain is gone.

But because it no longer has to be carried alone.

▶ *Related Toolkit: 5-Minute Reset Routines (Appendix B)*

Daily Anchor for Leading Anyway

Even when new storms emerge inside the existing ones, I remain anchored. I acknowledge the weight of compounded challenges without surrendering to them. My leadership holds steady as I tend to the urgent while preserving long-term stability. I am present, composed, and capable, even when layers of crisis press in.

> *Quietly or aloud, say after me:*
> **"I remain steady within the layers. My leadership does not fracture under pressure. I navigate complexity with calm strength."**

🌐 CHAPTER 10 LEADERSHIP SNAPSHOT 🌐

 FRAMEWORK IN ACTION

This chapter emphasizes three pillars of the *Global Leadership Framework*:

Emotional Centering: By equipping leaders to hold multiple emotional layers at once.

Collective Power and Voice: By validating internal team needs during external response.

Adaptive Leadership: By preparing leaders to navigate hidden breakdowns and shifting dynamics.

 KEY LEADERSHIP TAKEAWAYS

▷ Not all crises are visible. Emotional overload, silent conflict, and moral distress can compound external disasters.
▷ Internal breakdowns often mirror unspoken needs—naming them restores strength.
▷ Effective leaders know when to pause the task list to tend to the team.
▷ Psychological safety enables teams to surface hidden concerns without blame.
▷ Emotional regulation is not only individual—it is collective leadership work.

REFLECTIVE JOURNAL QUESTIONS

1. What secondary crises might be unfolding among my team or community right now?

2. How do I respond when emotional breakdowns disrupt task completion?

3. What practices help me notice and name invisible stressors in the system?

CULTURAL INSIGHT

In many regions, public expression of internal crisis is discouraged—or even punished. Leaders must create emotionally intelligent cultures where trauma and fatigue are normalized and addressed, not hidden. Chapter 10 encourages cross-cultural nuance when navigating unspoken emotional strain within high-stress environments.

USE THIS SECTION TO:

- Debrief teams when emotions are running high or morale is low
- Train leaders to recognize and respond to invisible stress signals
- Build support systems for caregiver burnout, survivor's guilt, or team fracture
- Introduce group rituals, circles, or pauses that make space for collective emotional care

Chapter 11

The Digital Storm — When the Headlines Become Your Trauma

How global disasters enter our nervous system through screens, even from afar

The Global Disaster You Cannot Turn Away From

In earlier generations, disasters were largely confined by geography. Today, with just a click, the entire world becomes a witness. Earlier in 2025, the United States experienced collective trauma when an American Airlines regional jet collided mid-air with a US Army helicopter over Washington, D.C. Sixty-seven lives were lost, and the incident unfolded publicly in full view of the nation's capital. As the FAA, NTSB, Congress, and aviation leaders began their investigations, people across the country followed every briefing, update, and unanswered question. It was not just the tragedy that affected people—it was the prolonged uncertainty that quietly added to the emotional weight already bearing down on the public.

> "Compassion fatigue is the emotional residue that builds when you hold space for others without replenishing yourself."

Just months later, another tragedy reverberated across the globe: a passenger plane crash in India claimed the lives of 241 people on board and 38 more on the ground. The crash left over 279 people dead. Though the incident occurred thousands of miles away for many viewers, it dominated screens from New York to Nairobi, from Mumbai to Melbourne. The images—twisted metal, grieving families, and emergency responders—arrived not in person, but through phones and laptops. In doing so, they entered our nervous systems. As the lone survivor emerged from the wreckage, the story deepened. Regulatory bodies like NASA, DGCA, FAA, and Boeing initiated parallel investigations while public scrutiny mounted on the Tata Group. The technical terms—flap deployment failure, gear malfunction—became part of a larger emotional narrative. This is what digital trauma often looks like. It is not just the tragedy—it is the slow, rolling story that continually revisits us through screens.

We Live in an Age of Collective Exposure

Earthquakes, floods, wildfires, mass shootings, conflicts, and famines pour directly into our palms. Children scroll past images of wounded civilians. Teachers receive news of school bombings before the school bell rings. Aid workers finish a shift only to see the next crisis unfold on their feed. Our bodies were not designed to absorb this much grief, this frequently, from this many places.

The emotional result? Fatigue without a clear cause. We feel worn down but cannot always name why. A creeping heaviness settles in. That's not weakness—it's exposure. It's what happens when every global event becomes a local wound, delivered in high-definition.

In this era of collective witnessing, leadership demands more than reaction. It requires discernment. You must recognize when your empathy has become saturated, when awareness has crossed into emotional overload. And you must

> "Boundaries are not a luxury. They are a survival tool."

138

act accordingly. The world will always need leaders—but it does not need you to dissolve in the process.

The Invisible Layer of Secondary Trauma

When disaster hits close to home, emotional shock makes sense. But when the grief builds over time—headline after headline—our nervous systems start to fray. Mental health professionals call this secondary or vicarious trauma. The images may not involve your community or your family, but your brain processes them as if they do. Your jaw tightens. Your heart rate spikes. Sleep becomes restless. You ask yourself, "Why am I so tired?" But your body already knows.

This layer of trauma often goes unnamed. We invalidate it because we were not physically there. But presence is no longer the requirement. Proximity is no longer the boundary. In the age of digital witnessing, the wound can arrive silently—through Wi-Fi.

Social Media as a Trauma Accelerator

In past decades, traumatic news was filtered—slowed down by television schedules and editorial decisions. Now, it is immediate and relentless. Graphic images auto-play. Anguished voices stream in real time. Emotional testimonies loop in your feed without warning. Social media is not designed to preserve your wellbeing—it is designed to hold your attention.

The more emotionally disturbing the content, the more it spreads. As a result, you may find yourself repeatedly exposed to the same devastation, long after the initial shock. And unlike a structured news cycle, social media never signals when to stop. You are left to draw your own boundaries—if you even realize they are needed.

You Do Not Have to Be There to Be Affected

This is the paradox of modern grief: you do not have to know the victims, or speak the language, or be in the same hemisphere to feel devastated. You may never set foot in Gaza, Uvalde, Kerala, or

Eastern Cape, but your body reacts as if you have. It is not imagined. It is not irrational. It is the cost of connection in a wired world.

Your nervous system does not care about geography. It responds to perceived danger and emotional distress. And in that way, digital proximity becomes real. A thousand miles away can still land in your chest like a stone.

The Leader's Dilemma: Carrying Global Grief

If you lead, you already carry the weight of those around you. But now, add to that the weight of the world. The war you cannot stop. The famine you cannot feed. The tragedies that fill your inbox and newsfeed. It creates a quiet undercurrent of sorrow beneath even your best leadership days.

This is where emotional integrity becomes essential. Not coldness. Not denial. But stewardship. A conscious choice to feel with clarity and set internal limits. You cannot hold all the pain, and you were never meant to.

Building Emotional Guardrails in a Digital Age

Create boundaries around your exposure the same way you would guard your physical safety. Steward your emotional energy like the resource it is.

- Curate your input. You don't have to click the video. You don't have to absorb the blow-by-blow.
- Set limits on when and how often you consume media.
- Name your emotions. Unnamed grief becomes stuck energy.
- Offer what is yours to give—locally, tangibly—and release the rest.
- Step away. Your nervous system needs silence, not just sleep.

When Digital Grief Quietly Accumulates

Digital grief is invisible. It builds with every scroll past a collapsed building, every headline of loss. Unlike traditional grief, it doesn't announce itself. It shows up as tension, short temper, forgetfulness, or apathy. The digital world gives no time for mourning. So you must create it.

Especially for leaders, the danger is subtle. You think you are fine because nothing happened "to you." But everything is happening around you—and your body knows. Emotional residue is real. It clouds judgment, dulls compassion, and makes you tired in ways rest cannot fix.

That is why boundary-setting is not avoidance—it is emotional hygiene. Discernment is not detachment—it is survival.

The Discipline of Guarding Your Emotional Gate

In this age, the leader must become a gatekeeper. Not to block empathy—but to protect its source. You cannot pour from a soul flooded with sorrow. That's not sustainable. That's collapse disguised as care.

Care, instead, with wisdom. Breathe before you click. Mute the noise. Walk outside. Light a candle. Do whatever restores you.

Closing Insight: You Cannot Carry It All

You do not serve others by drowning in sorrow you were never meant to carry. Keep your heart open, but ensure your boundaries are clear. Feel deeply. Grieve when necessary. Yet, let go of what does not belong to you. You are not called to bear the weight of the world; only to stand firm where you are.

"Leadership that lasts is not built on logistics—it's built on emotional sustainability."

There is a difference between compassion and collapse. Between holding space and holding responsibility for what is not yours to fix. In times of disaster, empathy can become a flood—rushing in so quickly that it leaves no room to breathe. That is when leadership must learn the art of letting go, without losing the sense of care.

You can honor pain without taking it all in. You can walk alongside people through the rubble without becoming rubble yourself. Boundaries are not barriers to love—they are its anchors. They protect your ability to stay present, wise, and well.

The world doesn't require you to bear everything. It needs you to hold yourself with strength, clarity, and compassion—so you can guide others home, even if just for a moment, to the feeling of safety once more.

▶   *Related Toolkit: Digital Grief Reflection Worksheet (Appendix J)*

Daily Anchor for Leading Anyway

I do not confuse my care with my capacity. My heart remains open, but my gate is guarded. I feel without drowning. I serve without collapsing. I am emotionally available for what I am meant to hold, and I release what does not belong to me.

> *Quietly or aloud, say after me:*
> **"I guard my emotional gate. I carry what is mine and release what is not. My peace protects my leadership."**

🌐 CHAPTER 11 LEADERSHIP SNAPSHOT 🌐

FRAMEWORK IN ACTION

This chapter strengthens three essential elements of the *Global Leadership Framework*:

Operational Clarity: By helping leaders manage communication flow and digital noise.

Emotional Centering: By addressing the emotional cost of hyper-connectivity during crisis.

Cultural Coordination: By guiding culturally sensitive digital messaging across diverse platforms.

KEY LEADERSHIP TAKEAWAYS

- In a digital storm, clarity is power—and restraint is leadership.
- Overcommunication without structure fuels confusion and emotional overwhelm.
- Misinformation spreads faster than verified facts in disaster contexts.
- Leaders must prioritize both emotional tone and cultural nuance in digital content.
- Silence, when intentional, can be a form of trust—not neglect.

REFLECTIVE JOURNAL QUESTIONS

1 How does my team manage digital fatigue in high-alert moments?

2 What systems can we put in place to verify and streamline digital messages?

3 Am I using technology to inform—or to overwhelm?

CULTURAL INSIGHT

In global crises, technology is both a lifeline and a liability. Misinformation travels across borders in seconds. Some cultures prefer in-person validation, while others rely heavily on mobile alerts. Chapter 11 pushes leaders to respect local tech habits and emotional thresholds while leading calmly in digital chaos.

USE THIS SECTION TO:

▶ Create communication SOPs (standard operating procedures) for crisis response
▶ Train leaders on misinformation management and emotional regulation in messaging
▶ Equip community organizations to balance urgency with clarity in digital spaces
▶ Design multilingual, trauma-informed communication plans across platforms

Chapter 12

The Leader's Survival Plan

The Hidden Cost of Leading Through Crisis

No one warns you how heavy it gets.

They tell you to lead, to coordinate, to show up for others. But they rarely speak of the cost—the weight of being the one others turn to while your own reserves quietly deplete. There's little preparation for what happens after the adrenaline fades, when the cameras leave and the needs remain.

This is the shadow side of crisis leadership: the slow erosion of self beneath the steady posture of strength.

> "People do not rise to the occasion— they fall to the level of their training."

You answer the questions. You make the decisions. You absorb the fear in the room and turn it into direction. But where do you place your own grief, your own fatigue, your own unraveling? In many cultures, especially those where caregiving roles disproportionately fall on women or community elders, leaders are expected to endure without revealing their cracks. This expectation, while arising from admiration, can become a silent prison.

Global crisis leaders—from refugee camp coordinators in Lebanon to school principals in storm-battered villages of the Philippines— carry the same invisible burden: holding others together while no one holds them. Over time, this leads to what some describe as compassion fatigue, though that terminology often falls short. It is not merely exhaustion; it is a deep, quiet ache that arises from carrying unspoken stories and unanswered questions long after the crisis has passed.

The cost is not just emotional; it is also physical. Leaders begin to lose sleep, appetite, clarity, and joy. They become short with loved ones and detached from themselves. Yet, they show up again—because the work matters, because people need them, and because it feels like no one else will.

But here is the truth: the strength you model doesn't have to mean self-abandonment. Leadership that sustains others must also allow for your own humanity. Otherwise, you will lead from depletion rather than from depth. The world doesn't need heroes who fade into burnout. It needs emotionally honest leaders who know how to pause, how to receive care, and how to return—not from compulsion, but from renewal.

This hidden cost can be acknowledged. It can be defined. And when it is, leaders across every culture, every crisis, and every context begin to rediscover something sacred: you are not only allowed to care for yourself—you are required to, if you intend to keep showing up for others.

What Compassion Fatigue Really Looks Like

It doesn't always arrive with fanfare. Sometimes it starts with fragmented sleep, a shorter fuse, and a sense of emotional numbness, even as you remain outwardly composed. You continue showing up, but the joy is gone. You're offering reassurance, even while quietly doubting your own capacity. The engine is still running, but it's fueled by fumes—and you call it service.

This isn't weakness. It's compassion fatigue. And it's real.

Compassion fatigue is the emotional residue that builds up when you create emotional safety for others without replenishing yourself. It accumulates when you carry pain that isn't yours, absorb sorrow you cannot fix, and bear witness to suffering—again and again—without time or tools to process your own.

Case Example
Frontline Exhaustion in Haiti

Following the 2021 earthquake in southern Haiti, a local nurse in Les Cayes worked 16-hour days treating burn victims and crush injuries. When aid finally arrived, she collapsed from dehydration and exhaustion. Her story became a national reminder that local responders often bear the greatest emotional toll—and that their well-being must be part of the response, not an afterthought.

In post-disaster environments, fatigue is common. The constant urgency of recovery can lead leaders to believe that movement equals effectiveness. However, leadership isn't just about logistics; it's about longevity. And longevity relies on the leader's protection as well.

Recognizing the Early Signals

There is no exact formula for preventing burnout. However, there are signs: emotional detachment, growing resentment, and a persistent belief that rest is selfish. These are not failures; they are messages. Like any signal, they deserve attention—not shame. Sustainable leadership begins with listening to your internal alerts before they turn into alarms.

When your body flinches at the sound of another request, when your heart sinks at the start of the day, or when you find yourself going numb just to get through—these are early indicators that something sacred is being overdrawn. Too often, leaders interpret these signals as weakness and push harder. But resilience is not about overriding your needs; it's about respecting them early enough to restore what is fading.

"Preparedness isn't just future-focused—it's the decision to learn, evolve, and lead differently next time."

The most grounded leaders are not those who never falter. They are the ones who pause, recalibrate, and return—not only to the mission but also to themselves. Burnout rarely arrives all at once; it creeps in quietly, disguised as duty. Acknowledging it is not a sign of failure; it is an act of wisdom.

Boundaries Are Essential for Survival, Not Selfishness

Boundaries are not a luxury; they are a survival tool. They delineate the line between your responsibilities and those of others. They grant you permission to say "no" without guilt. They empower you to delegate without overfunctioning. They emphasize that being constantly available doesn't demonstrate greater commitment—it leads to depletion.

If you were raised in environments where self-sacrifice was normalized—or even spiritualized—boundaries may feel unnatural. But let this be clear: rest is not abandonment. A pause is not betrayal. A breath is not failure. It's wisdom. Because you are part of the community too. And your exhaustion—especially when unexpressed—has a ripple effect. It shapes how you lead, how you relate, and how safe others feel in your presence.

> "The most resilient leaders are not the ones who knew the most before the storm. They are the ones who evolved."

Rhythms That Make Recovery Sustainable

You cannot hold every loss. You cannot be present for every need. You cannot plan, feel, decide, and carry it all without something breaking. Let it not be you.

Recovery leadership requires rhythm. Incorporate short pauses into your day. Five minutes of stillness between tasks. A moment of hydration. A gentle reset. Allow someone else to lead, even if briefly. Choose rest before collapse. Reflect before resentment. Prioritize human needs over heroic illusions.

Case Example
Scheduled Pauses in a South African Field Camp

During cholera containment efforts in KwaZulu-Natal, field workers implemented daily "reorientation breaks"—ten minutes every four hours to stretch, breathe, and reconnect. Leadership encouraged silence or laughter but discouraged problem-solving. These micro-breaks minimized team conflicts and burnout during the 14-day rotation.

An Invitation Back to Yourself

If you are already at your limit—burned out, bitter, ashamed—this is your invitation back to yourself. You do not have to start over. You only have to start from here, with awareness and compassion. Begin where your feet are. Begin with the breath you have left. You are not behind—you are arriving.

Your worth is not defined by your output. Your value is not measured by how much you can endure. Leadership that arises from depletion is unsustainable. However, leadership rooted in self-return—honoring your own needs, rhythms, and capacity—becomes a source that can nourish others.

You can lead and heal simultaneously. You can respect your limits without rejecting your purpose. You can change direction, slow down, or pause completely—and still be powerful. The invitation is not to forsake your calling, but to respond to it from a place that does not forsake you. Let this moment be the threshold—not of failure, but of your own reclamation.

Case Example
When the Work Is the Weight — The Hidden
Burnout of DEI Leaders (2024–2025)

In the aftermath of global protests and corporate reckonings, thousands of organizations committed to enhancing diversity, equity, and inclusion. Yet by late 2024, a new and often overlooked crisis emerged—not among those being served, but among those providing the service.

Across corporate America, DEI leaders began to exit their roles at an alarming rate. According to a 2024 Seramount survey, 69 percent of Chief Diversity Officers reported experiencing significant burnout. These cases were not isolated. The same leaders who had been tasked with facilitating healing and inclusion were now reporting that they felt isolated themselves. Public-facing, emotionally demanding, and often under-resourced, they were being asked to lead systemic change—without the necessary systemic support.

Many described feeling emotionally drained, caught between organizational pressure, public expectations, and personal identity. They were asked to listen to painful employee experiences while concealing their own, to advocate for bold change while being sidelined from decision-making. Despite holding leadership positions, they were often excluded from strategy discussions or budget allocation. One executive shared anonymously, "I am exhausted from being both the spokesperson and the sponge. I absorb everyone's pain, but I have nowhere to put my own."

By early 2025, over two-thirds of surveyed DEI leaders rated their personal well-being as below average. Only 18 percent reported getting even seven hours of sleep each night. The positions they were hired for had become unsustainable—not due to a lack of passion, but due to a lack of protection. Some left feeling burned out, while others felt disillusioned. What was intended to be a movement had turned into a revolving door.

This is the unseen cost of crisis leadership: when the very work becomes the burden. It is not only natural disasters or military conflicts that drain leaders; it is also the emotional labor performed in boardrooms, Zoom meetings, and employee forums. It is a crisis that arrives disguised as a calendar invite but feels like a reckoning of identity. And it reminds us that regardless of how noble the mission, leaders cannot endure the impact without internal recovery systems.

Closing Insight: Your Well-being Is the Strategy

Leadership is not determined by how much pain you can endure. It is demonstrated in how wisely you safeguard the vessel carrying you. Your nervous system is not separate from the mission; it is part of the framework. When it fails, so does clarity. When it is nurtured, you provide others with a stable place to land.

Rest is not a retreat from responsibility; it is the recalibration that makes wise leadership possible. Your boundaries are not signs of weakness; they are evidence of emotional maturity. When you give yourself permission to pause, you model a new kind of strength—one that does not require collapse to prove commitment.

In times of crisis, your very presence becomes part of the atmosphere. If that presence is calm, grounded, and emotionally whole, it does more than lead—it stabilizes. It reminds others that something steady still exists. It creates space for coherence amid chaos.

Incorporate your survival into the strategy. Ensure your care encompasses yourself—not as an afterthought, but as a fundamental aspect of sustainable leadership.

The work will continue, and so must you.

▶ *Related Toolkit: Solo Reset Routine (Appendix B)*

Daily Anchor for Leading Anyway

My leadership requires care for both others and myself. I am not immune to depletion, and I refuse to sacrifice my own well-being in the name of performance. I build rhythms that sustain me. I preserve my capacity to serve by honoring rest, reflection, and recalibration as non-negotiable parts of my leadership.

Quietly or aloud, say after me:
"I protect my capacity. My leadership is strengthened by care, rhythm, and intentional restoration."

🌎 CHAPTER 12 LEADERSHIP SNAPSHOT 🌎

 FRAMEWORK IN ACTION

This chapter grounds itself in three central components of the *Global Leadership Framework*:

Emotional Centering: By emphasizing sustainable leadership through boundaries, rest, and emotional honesty.

Adaptive Leadership: By allowing leaders to pivot without shame or collapse.

Collective Power and Voice: By modeling self-care so others feel permission to do the same.

 KEY LEADERSHIP TAKEAWAYS

▶ You cannot lead others well if you have abandoned yourself.
▶ Rest, boundaries, and honest emotional reflection are not luxuries—they are lifelines.
▶ A leader's nervous system sets the tone for the entire response team.
▶ Knowing when to pause, delegate, or downshift is wisdom—not weakness.
▶ Survival plans protect your clarity, your body, and your calling.

REFLECTIVE JOURNAL QUESTIONS

1 How do I respond to my own exhaustion—deny it, hide it, or name it?

2 What systems can I implement now to support long-term emotional sustainability?

3 Who do I trust to hold space for me when I need to regroup?

CULTURAL INSIGHT

In many cultures, leaders are expected to endure without complaint. But global disasters have revealed a universal truth: emotionally depleted leaders create emotionally unsafe environments. Chapter 12 affirms that emotional resilience is a shared responsibility, and that modeling self-care creates space for collective sustainability.

USE THIS SECTION TO:

- Encourage high-performing leaders to build survival strategies proactively
- Train team leads to identify burnout signals early
- Normalize rest, rotation, and emotional support in crisis response teams
- Design personal and team-level care protocols for surge events

Chapter 13

Beyond the Storm

Restoration or Readiness?

Disasters do not arrive with invitations. They appear without warning, disrupt without permission, and leave behind questions no emergency manual can fully answer. But in the stillness after a crisis, one decision always remains: Will we simply restore what was—or prepare for what may come?

For communities in high-risk regions, the next storm is not a matter of if, but when. Yet few are taught how to prepare beyond logistics. We store bottled water, check forecasts, and run drills. However, we often forget to reinforce the human infrastructure—the relationships, emotional regulation, cultural trust, and team reflexes that define how a community survives.

This is the heart of true recovery: not just rebuilding structures, but reinforcing people.

> "Hope is not the absence of pain. It is the quiet decision to keep moving forward."

Reimagining Preparedness

Disaster preparation involves more than just checklists and supplies; it includes emotional rehearsals, a shared language, and mental clarity. It requires building relational trust before a crisis hits. It necessitates strengthening team communication, identifying emotional anchors, and practicing decision-making under pressure—when the stakes are imaginary, so that when they become real, the body remembers how to respond.

Preparedness is not only logistical—it is profoundly human. In every region of the world, the success of response efforts is influenced not just by resources, but by the readiness of mind, spirit, and connection. People do not rise to the occasion; they fall to the level of their training—and to the degree of trust they possess in those beside them.

The quality of leadership during the next emergency will reflect what was practiced before it ever arrived. Furthermore, what is practiced must extend beyond protocols—it must encompass compassion, clarity, and cultural awareness.

The Wisdom of Looking Back

We begin by remembering, not to dwell, but to learn. Each disaster leaves a trail of lessons—some painful, some profound. Those who lead well in the future are those who dare to look back honestly.

Ask yourself and your community:

- What broke down last time?
- Who carried too much?
- Where were the gaps in communication, clarity, or inclusion?
- What rituals or cultural anchors provided resilience?
- Who emerged unexpectedly as a source of strength?

Wise leadership captures these reflections and transforms them into systems—not rooted in fear, but grounded in humility and care.

Preparedness isn't about predicting every threat. It's about developing the ability to respond—not with panic, but with presence. This starts with the courage to look backward, allowing us to move forward with intention.

Case Example
Debriefing Circles in Haiti

After the 2010 earthquake, a women's cooperative in Léogâne, Haiti, began hosting weekly debriefing circles. They gathered beneath tarps, lit candles, and openly shared what they learned, feared, and remembered. These meetings became the foundation of a local disaster plan—one based on cultural memory and collective wisdom.

Training for What Cannot Be Predicted

You cannot simulate every emergency. But you can strengthen your team's reflexes. Leadership under pressure is not about having a perfect script—it is about being prepared enough to improvise with steadiness, compassion, and clarity.

This preparation occurs well in advance of a crisis—when the environment is still calm, allowing time to build trust, test communication patterns, and create space for reflection. The goal is not to rehearse specific events but to foster adaptive thinking and emotional resilience within the team.

Examples of this type of training vary across regions and roles, but all emphasize emotional intelligence, cultural awareness, and clear communication. One exercise might involve role-playing how to manage the rapid spread of misinformation—when partial truths or panic begin to spread

"You are not asked to manufacture hope—only to keep enough light present so people remember where to walk."

faster than verified facts. Another may include a guided debrief among school staff members, exploring ways to support students who have been displaced or emotionally affected, particularly through a lens of cultural sensitivity and trauma-informed care. In some communities, leaders facilitate forums where local traditions and mental health frameworks converge, creating a shared language for healing and restoration. Perhaps most importantly, training must also encompass contingency planning—designing a structure that considers who steps in when the designated leader becomes emotionally or physically unavailable. This ensures leadership is a shared capacity, not a single point of failure. In many global contexts, informal leadership holds as much influence as official titles. Acknowledging and involving these leaders in this preparation not only enhances outcomes but also fosters community cohesion.

These exercises are not "extras." They are acts of leadership foresight. They are rehearsals in emotional integrity, clarity under stress, and trust-building when nothing is certain. They develop muscle memory—and that memory becomes calm under pressure. In the absence of predictability, practiced presence becomes your most valuable asset.

The Power of Adaptability

Preparedness also requires permission—permission to change, to revise the plan, to update roles, to grow. The most resilient leaders are not those who knew the most before the storm. They are the ones who evolved, who listened, and who let go of rigidity in favor of wisdom.

> "Hope is not a feeling we wait for. It is a muscle we use."

Adaptability is not a passive reaction; it is an active choice. It involves letting go of the illusion that the original plan will remain effective in every circumstance. It requires recognizing what no longer works—even if it once did—and having the humility to pivot. In disaster response, those who adapt quickly do not discard structure; they maintain what is most important while altering everything else.

Rigid systems tend to break under pressure. Flexible leaders bend without losing their integrity. They adjust their tone, methods, and even expectations—not because they are uncertain, but because they are attuned. Adaptability honors reality. It responds in real time instead of clinging to outdated ideals.

In the field, adaptability manifests as recalibrating a response plan. At the desk, it requires shifting timelines when trauma slows progress. Emotionally, it entails pausing when urgency leads to overwhelm. The leaders who navigate crises most effectively are those who remain grounded in purpose yet open in approach.

Adaptability is not the absence of preparation—it is its evolution.

Honoring Cultural Strengths

Many communities already embody resilience through seasonal gatherings, storytelling circles, prayer walks, and cultural ceremonies. These practices are more than traditions; they are powerful tools. They transmit strength through ritual, create a sense of belonging, and reinforce identity.

Do not replace them with "efficiency." Rather, integrate and elevate them. When you honor what is sacred, you deepen readiness without erasing cultural roots.

Case Example
Story Walks in Kerala, India

In a coastal village in Kerala, elders and children participate in monthly "memory walks," recounting past monsoons and survival lessons. These walks are integrated into school activities and also serve as cultural and emotional preparedness. These rituals preserve strength and teach resilience.

Simple Structures, Deep Impact

Still, structure has its place. A laminated contact list, a visible supply rotation chart, and a shared emergency script are examples of effective tools. These do not require major funding—but they create calm.

Continuity soothes the nervous system. A child who knows what to expect, an elder who understands their role, and a community that communicates a shared language during stressful times—these are subtle yet powerful forms of protection.

Emotional Memory and Collective Resilience

Preparedness also includes emotional memory—not as a trigger, but as a resource. Children who remember being comforted are less fearful the next time. Volunteers who saw you lead with composure trust your voice during future chaos. Elders who felt respected provide stability to those around them.

You are not just preparing logistics; you are shaping how memory is encoded.

You are building resilience across generations.

Case Example
Puerto Rican Leadership Post-Maria

After Hurricane Maria devastated Puerto Rico, formal aid stalled. In response, local leaders transformed schools into clinics and organized supply lines through WhatsApp. Elders received insulin, rainwater was collected from rooftops, and communities coordinated their own care long before external systems recovered. It was grassroots governance in motion—urgent, emotional, and deeply human.

2025 Snapshot: The Leaders History May Forget

While global attention often shifts quickly, many communities remain trapped in ongoing cycles of trauma long after the cameras have left. In 2025, as some nations stabilized, others descended further into humanitarian crises. From refugee camps in the Middle East to tent cities in Haiti to flooded villages in East Africa, unsung leaders emerged daily—organizing food lines, managing medical triage, soothing displaced children, and offering fragile hope where little remained. These were not appointed leaders. They were neighbors, mothers, students, and elders who chose to support others through the unrecorded hours of history.

2023 Snapshot: The Flood That Swept Away a City (Libya, Derna Flood)

In September 2023, torrential rains overwhelmed aging dams near Derna, Libya, causing a catastrophic flood that swept entire neighborhoods into the sea. Thousands died within hours, their homes erased as water engulfed streets and buildings in the darkness of night. When daylight broke, survivors stood among the wreckage with no clear leadership structure in place.

Political divisions delayed international response efforts. In that void, local residents organized search parties, distributed food, created makeshift shelters, and coordinated the recovery of bodies. Medical students treated injured neighbors. Shopkeepers converted businesses into supply stations. Grief was everywhere—but so was resolve. Their leadership was not born from training; it emerged from the unbearable reality that no one else was coming fast enough. And still, they stood.

Closing Insight: Quiet Leadership, Lasting Impact

There will be no applause for this kind of preparation. No headlines for building before the next disaster. But this is the work that matters. This is the leadership that saves lives—because it shapes how people feel, think, and act when everything else falls apart.

You cannot prevent every loss.

You cannot predict every risk.

But you can prepare people.

And in doing so, you turn reaction into resilience.

You are not just leading through disaster.

You are preparing your people to survive the next one—together.

▶   *Related Toolkit: Institutional Memory Logs and Recovery Ritual Templates (Appendix E)*

Daily Anchor for Leading Anyway

Storms do not define me. I acknowledge what I've endured, but I refuse to live anchored to the past. My leadership is not rooted in survival alone, but in renewal. I step forward carrying wisdom, not wounds. Beyond the storm, I build with clarity, gratitude, and quiet strength.

> *Quietly or aloud, say after me:*
> **"I am not what I survived. I lead from wisdom, not from wounds. The future is open before me."**

CHAPTER 13 LEADERSHIP SNAPSHOT

FRAMEWORK IN ACTION

This chapter anchors itself in three pillars of the *Global Leadership Framework*:

Cultural Coordination: By centering the long-term needs and cultural rhythms of affected communities.

Collective Power and Voice: By ensuring those most impacted continue to shape recovery.

Operational Clarity: By building systems for sustainable support beyond the immediate crisis.

KEY LEADERSHIP TAKEAWAYS

- Disasters end in the media long before they end for the community.
- The real leadership begins when urgency fades—and people still need to be seen.
- Long-term trust is built through consistent presence, not temporary aid.
- True recovery honors cultural rhythms, not outside timelines.
- Emotional presence is just as vital during rebuilding as it is during rescue.

REFLECTIVE JOURNAL QUESTIONS

1 Am I prepared to stay engaged after the cameras leave?

2 How can I ensure that recovery timelines honor—not over-ride—community needs?

3 What does long-term solidarity look like in my leadership role?

CULTURAL INSIGHT

Globally, many communities have faced repeated abandonment by external aid once the "moment" passes. Chapter 13 challenges the performance-based model of help and invites leaders into relational recovery—where local wisdom, not external speed, sets the tone for healing.

USE THIS SECTION TO:

▶ Plan follow-up structures for NGOs, schools, and government agencies

▶ Develop long-term leadership strategies for communities in rebuilding phases

▶ Design recovery benchmarks that include emotional, cultural, and economic repair

▶ Train leaders to shift from emergency response to sustained relational presence

Chapter 14

Hope Is a Skill

The Unspoken Question

After the storm has passed, after the losses have been counted, after the systems have been stretched thin, something quieter begins to emerge—a question not always spoken aloud, but felt in the body, in the eyes, in the rhythm of everyday life:

> **"Leadership after disaster is emotional design."**

Will we be okay?

Not just physically. Not just logistically. But emotionally. Spiritually. Collectively.

This question lingers in shelter lines and schoolyards. In faith gatherings and neighborhood meetings. In whispered prayers and silent commutes. It is asked by children in their drawings, by elders in their pauses, by leaders in their private moments of doubt.

It is a question of more than survival. It is a plea for reassurance that what was shaken can be steady again. That what was broken can be honored, if not restored. That even if nothing goes back to how it was, we will find a way forward—together.

Leaders do not need to have a definitive answer. What matters is that they do not ignore the question. The courage to name uncertainty, to offer presence instead of promises, becomes the beginning of emotional repair.

To the unspoken question, *Will we be okay?*—your grounded presence, your compassion, and your steady leadership whisper something powerful in return:

"We are not alone. And we are finding our way."

When Morale Becomes the Next Emergency

This is the point in recovery when morale becomes the next emergency. Not because people are ungrateful, but because they're exhausted. They've been running on adrenaline and urgency. Even with shelter and supplies, many still feel disconnected, disoriented, and uncertain about what comes next. The buildings may be standing, but trust is shattered. Community feels distant. And hope—if mentioned at all—seems too abstract to grasp.

That's why hope must be taught like any other leadership tool: not romanticized, not forced, but cultivated, practiced, and protected.

What Hope Really Means

Hope is not the absence of pain. It is not a performance of positivity. It is the quiet decision to keep moving forward, even when nothing feels certain. It is not blind optimism or forced smiles in the face of loss. Hope does not deny devastation—it rises alongside it. It sits in the ashes and still chooses to believe in tomorrow.

Hope is the teacher reopening a school with only half the building intact. It is the community leader gathering neighbors when no formal help has arrived. It is the elder planting seeds in soil that has already endured floods, fires, or wars. It is the choice to believe that rebuilding is possible—not because we ignore what happened, but because we refuse to let it have the final word.

Hope is not loud. It does not always arrive with fanfare. Often, it enters quietly—in the form of presence, persistence, or a single small act of care. In crisis leadership, hope is not just an emotion; it is a strategy. It is what enables people to keep showing up, keep trying, and keep healing.

True hope honors pain without being defined by it. It allows space for grief, and then gently reminds us: this is not the end of the story.

The Work of Post-Crisis Meaning-Making

In trauma-informed recovery, this shift is known as post-crisis meaning-making. It refers to the phase when people begin to ask not just "What happened?" but "Who are we now because of it?" This phase establishes the foundation for long-term resilience, and it cannot be rushed. However, it also cannot be overlooked. When communities neglect this phase, hopelessness creeps in, fragmentation increases, blame surfaces, and people withdraw or fight over what cannot be undone.

As a leader, your role is not to manufacture hope. Your role is to keep enough light present so people remember where to walk.

Rituals and Small Restorations

This can be achieved through small rituals—gatherings that honor both what was lost and what still remains. Moments of storytelling, where people can remember their strength. Spaces where children are allowed to play again. Places where elders are invited to speak. Routines that feel safe and familiar, even in unfamiliar environments.

Sometimes, it's as simple as acknowledging progress. Not in a way that dismisses grief, but in a way that reminds people: "We're not where we were." A rebuilt home, a reopened school, and a community garden planted on cleared debris—these are not symbolic acts. They are declarations of continuity, of life choosing to root again.

Case Example
Food as Dignity in Haiti

In the aftermath of the 2010 earthquake, women in Port-au-Prince converted church courtyards into makeshift kitchens. With limited supplies, they fed entire neighborhoods while singing hymns and telling stories. These acts of care were more than nourishment—they reminded people of their worth. In disaster, hope often arrives not through words, but through service with soul.

Case Example
Hurricane Recovery in Jamaica

In 2020, Hurricane Zeta caused widespread damage in parts of Jamaica. While government agencies coordinated large-scale recovery efforts, it was often local neighborhood councils and church networks that provided day-to-day care. Pastors and community health workers organized food lines, coordinated medication distribution for the elderly, and created safe spaces for children in affected communities. Their steady presence not only addressed immediate needs but also preserved community dignity in the face of overwhelming loss. Long after the storm passed, these grassroots leaders continued to support emotional recovery.

Case Example
Gardens of Renewal in Dominica

After Hurricane Maria devastated Dominica in 2017, women in rural villages began planting "healing gardens" using salvaged herbs, seeds, and cuttings from damaged land. These gardens became more than a source of food—they restored rhythm and dignity to daily life. The scent of mint, basil, and lemongrass filled the air, signaling that nourishment—both physical and emotional—was returning. As neighbors tended the soil together, these quiet acts of renewal helped rebuild not only community health, but also hope.

Case Example
Cyclone Recovery in Fiji

In 2016, Cyclone Winston devastated large areas of Fiji, displacing thousands across numerous outer islands. While international aid provided emergency relief, village chiefs, known as Turaga-ni-Koro, played a pivotal role in stabilizing local communities. Elders organized communal rebuilding efforts, coordinated rotating food preparation teams, and used traditional storytelling and song to comfort children who had lost homes and family members. Rooted in indigenous cultural resilience, their leadership fostered emotional stability, preserved identity, and maintained social

> "Restoration must include rhythm— predictability, respect, clarity."

cohesion long after external agencies had departed. In many island nations, leadership is upheld as much through generational wisdom as through formal systems.

Rebuilding Trust and Emotional Infrastructure

Hope is also rebuilt through relational trust. When leaders show up consistently, when promises are kept, when decisions are communicated with transparency, and when people feel seen—not as data points, but as neighbors, parents, children, caregivers, and survivors. In places where trust was already fragile, this takes time. But it can be done: one honest conversation at a time, one conflict navigated with care, and one team meeting where people are allowed to speak without judgment.

Beauty as a Lifeline

Do not underestimate the role of beauty in recovery. Music, color, art, and laughter are not luxuries—they are lifelines. They reawaken the senses after long periods of numbness and remind people that joy is still possible; that life is not only functional but worth living.

Case Example
Art Therapy in Post-War Ukraine

In the wake of the 2022 Russian invasion of Ukraine, cities like Bucha and Irpin became synonymous with trauma. But amid the rubble and uncertainty, something unexpected began to emerge—color. In Kyiv and surrounding areas, local artists, therapists, and volunteers launched mobile art therapy clinics for children and the elderly. Bomb shelters transformed into galleries of crayon murals. Scarred buildings were adorned with hopeful paintings. Community workshops invited people to paint their grief, sculpt their memories, and sing through their sorrow.

One child, just nine years old, painted sunflowers sprouting from broken tanks. An elderly woman, displaced from Kharkiv, found herself singing lullabies to strangers during an open-mic healing night at a shelter. These expressions didn't erase the trauma—but they softened its edge. The act of creating beauty amid devastation became a form of resistance, resilience, and relief in its own right.

Beauty gave them breath when language failed. It restored dignity when systems collapsed. And in a country still counting its losses, beauty became a lifeline—a quiet, steady assertion that life was still worth experiencing.

Your Role: Steward, Not Source

And if you feel uncertain about hope yourself—if your own spirit is still wading through grief—know that you do not have to be the source of it. You only need to be a steward.

You are not required to ignite hope in every room you enter. But you can protect it. You can clear space for it to breathe, even when you are not sure it will arrive. You can choose to hold the door open—quietly, patiently—so that when others begin to glimpse the future again, they find that hope has not been shut out.

This is the quiet role of the leader after the storm: not to provide all the answers, but to preserve the conditions where healing and belief can return in their own time.

You are a steward of possibility, not perfection. Of safety, not certainty. Of presence, not pressure. That is more than enough.

Even in your own fatigue, your choice to stay steady creates room for others to hope again. And in doing so, you often rediscover your own.

> "The emotional atmosphere you build will outlast every tent, budget, or speech."

Hope Is a Practice

Some days, your leadership may embody structure. Other days, it may reflect softness. Both elements are essential. Both contribute to building hope.

Hope is not a feeling we wait for; it is a muscle we use, a skill we practice, and a gift we offer—not because everything is okay, but because we believe that one day, with enough care, time, and courage, it can be better.

Closing Insight: You Are Part of That Future

You are part of that future. Every time you rebuild with dignity, lead with empathy, speak with clarity, or rest without guilt, you make the next day more attainable.

You are not just recovering from what happened—you are helping define what comes next.

Your presence becomes part of the healing architecture. Your decisions shape the culture that future generations will inherit. Your steadiness today becomes tomorrow's memory of safety.

That is what leadership looks like after the storm. Not a return to what was, but a reimagining of what could be—with more compassion, more wisdom, and more humanity.

That is what makes it worth surviving.

And that is what makes you essential.

▶ *Related Toolkit: Community Ritual Templates (Appendix E)*

Daily Anchor for Leading Anyway

Hope is not something I wait to feel. It is a discipline I choose to practice. Even when outcomes remain uncertain, I exercise the muscle of hope — believing, envisioning, and preparing for what can be. My hope is not naive; it is rooted, grounded, and resilient.

> *Quietly or aloud, say after me:*
> **"I choose hope as a discipline. My hope is strong, steady, and rooted in what is possible."**

🌐 CHAPTER 14 LEADERSHIP SNAPSHOT 🌐

 FRAMEWORK IN ACTION

This chapter integrates three critical dimensions of the *Global Leadership Framework*:

> **Emotional Centering**: By framing hope not as a feeling, but as a resilient leadership practice.

> **Collective Power and Voice**: By empowering communities to name their own futures.

> **Adaptive Leadership**: By teaching leaders how to cultivate emotional momentum through uncertainty.

KEY LEADERSHIP TAKEAWAYS

▷ Hope is not passive—it is practiced. It requires language, vision, and repetition.

▷ In the aftermath of trauma, hope must be modeled before it can be felt.

▷ Emotional leadership involves helping people imagine life beyond survival.

▷ Tending to imagination is just as important as tending to logistics.

▷ Skilled leaders help communities speak of what is possible before they fully believe it.

REFLECTIVE JOURNAL QUESTIONS

1 How do I speak hope without bypassing pain?

2 What does emotional reconstruction look like after the visible damage is addressed?

3 What language do I use that either builds or blocks belief in a better future?

CULTURAL INSIGHT

In many cultural traditions, hope is passed down through storytelling, song, prayer, or communal rituals. Chapter 14 reminds leaders that hope is not always loud or logical—it often speaks in quiet repetition, through symbols, gestures, and shared vision.

USE THIS SECTION TO:

▷ Train leaders to embed emotional reconstruction in every phase of disaster recovery

- Develop messaging and rituals that help communities reclaim belief in their future
- Help teams practice language that balances honesty and encouragement
- Reframe hope as an active skill, not just an outcome

Part V

Designing What Comes Next

Recovery is not just about restoring what was lost—it is about reimagining what can be built.

After a disaster, the temptation is to return to what feels familiar. But "normal" often included broken systems, overlooked needs, and fragile structures that could not withstand the crisis in the first place. This section invites you to move beyond immediate relief and into long-term transformation.

In the island nation of Tuvalu, where rising sea levels threaten permanent displacement, community leaders have begun preparing citizens for eventual resettlement—while preserving ancestral identity. Instead of focusing solely on physical relocation, village elders gather with youth to teach cultural songs, family histories, and language preservation rituals. Their leadership reveals what many already know: emotional grounding and cultural continuity are essential forms of disaster leadership—long before the final wave arrives.

What kind of leadership culture will take root once the noise settles? What emotional framework will guide the rebuilding process? How do you lead in communities that remain displaced—physically, spiritually, or generationally? And how do you honor the faith traditions, personal convictions, and deeper questions that arise in the quiet aftermath?

These chapters guide you in designing leadership for what comes next. They help you preserve memory, identity, and meaning as you build systems—not just to help, but to heal. You will be called to lead with both emotional intelligence and spiritual integrity, developing recovery plans that include belonging, not just shelter.

Because true rebuilding does not begin with materials. It begins with mindset. And your leadership becomes the soil in which resilience can either flourish—or fade.

You are not just ending a crisis.

You are shaping what comes after.

Chapter 15

The Emotional Framework for Recovery

Signal or Noise: Navigating Digital Coordination and Misinformation

The Double-Edged Tool of Crisis Communication

In the aftermath of a disaster, communication moves quickly—often faster than supplies or formal briefings. A single message, voice note, or forwarded post can reach hundreds in seconds, shifting the emotional atmosphere before the facts even settle. Phones buzz. Alerts ping. Group chats flood with questions and assumptions. In the blur of urgency, the line between signal and noise becomes dangerously thin.

"Displacement is not just about where people go. It's about what they carry."

This represents the double-edged nature of digital tools in a crisis. On one hand, they can save lives—facilitating check-ins, mobilizing aid, and alerting people to danger. On the other, they can distort reality, escalate panic, or discredit efforts meant to help. Leaders must now respond to two storms: the one on the ground and the one online.

Tone Over Detail: Why Voice Still Matters

Digital communication does not exist in a vacuum. Every message lands in an emotional landscape already shaped by trauma, urgency, and loss. That's why tone is as important as content. When uncertainty is high, people seek steadiness over specifics. A calm, grounded voice note often does more to alleviate panic than a detailed, text-heavy update. When the source is trusted—when the person speaking has shown consistency, emotional presence, and local understanding—people are more likely to pause, breathe, and follow the guidance.

Repairing the Emotional Aftershocks of Misinformation

Yet trust is fragile in the digital age. A single forwarded rumor can unravel hours of coordinated effort. One misinterpreted directive can mislead volunteers or provoke anger among families that are already distressed. In many communities—from storm-hit Louisiana to earthquake-affected Nepal to flood-ravaged rural Australia—local leaders have found themselves engaged in emotional repair not only from the disaster itself but also from the confusion caused by viral misinformation.

Rhythm and Containment in Digital Spaces

> "Leadership in displacement begins with listening to what people didn't get to bring."

The problem is not always malice; more often, it's fear. People share what they believe might help. They fill gaps with guesses and repost before reading closely. In WhatsApp groups and online forums, a well-intentioned alert can turn into a full-blown false alarm. As a leader, your role is not to shame those who panic but to gently re-anchor the conversation. This may require repeating yourself, offering the same clarification in different formats,

178

and allowing people to ask again. Leadership in this space is not about correcting quickly—it's about restoring trust slowly.

In digital spaces, structure matters. Unmoderated group chats can easily become emotional dumping grounds, where grief and confusion spiral unchecked. One way to lead is by modeling digital containment. Instead of silencing voices, offer rhythm. Create a space for emotional expression without allowing it to consume the group's focus. Re-center conversations with calm summaries: "Here's what we know right now." "This plan is still unfolding—please hold questions while we confirm details." "Take a breath—we're going step by step."

Case Example
Silence and Story in South Africa

After community flooding in Eastern Cape, recovery groups began each meeting with a minute of silence. Then, instead of jumping straight into logistics, they opened space for storytelling—personal memories, loss, and cultural rituals. This emotional framing transformed coordination sessions into healing circles, anchoring the work in shared meaning before movement.

Case Example
Post-Flood Healing in Mozambique

After devastating floods swept through central Mozambique in 2019, formal aid was delayed by infrastructure breakdowns. In response, women from several villages began holding weekly storytelling circles under trees. These gatherings provided space for survivors—especially elders and mothers—to grieve, share survival strategies, and sing ancestral songs. The emotional weight of loss was made lighter through ritual, rhythm, and cultural memory. What emerged was not just coping—but reconnection to identity, dignity, and shared strength.

Case Example
Youth Leadership in Lebanon

Following the Beirut port explosion in 2020, local university students mobilized rapidly—not with supplies, but with presence. They set up mobile mental health tents throughout impacted neighborhoods. Instead of formal therapy, they simply sat, listened, and validated experiences. For many survivors, this was the first time someone acknowledged their fear and pain without rushing to fix it. These pop-up listening posts became a turning point in emotional recovery, offering communal trust in a city that felt deeply betrayed.

Culturally Grounded Emotional Rituals

Recovery cannot be measured by structural rebuild alone. In many parts of the world, healing begins not with words but with ritual. Song, silence, shared meals, prayer walks, and intergenerational gatherings hold a different kind of power—restorative, anchoring, and identity-affirming. These expressions of emotional continuity remind people they are still whole, even when surrounded by loss. Effective crisis leadership does not replace these moments. It makes room for them. Because where there is cultural memory, there is healing capacity.

Returning to the Framework

This is where the emotional framework must live beyond theory. *Emotional Centering* allows you to regulate yourself before leading others. *Presence* helps you ground a room even when the outcome remains unclear. And *Long-Term Meaning and Recovery* is not just about rebuilding systems—it is about helping communities rediscover who they are. Each layer, when honored, becomes a thread in the fabric of healing. This is the unseen work of recovery—the emotional scaffolding beneath every roof rebuilt and every life restored.

Modeling Presence— Even Through a Screen

Sometimes, clarity comes from how you present yourself rather than from what you say. A leader who speaks calmly, avoids dramatic language, and acknowledges uncertainty without offering false comfort becomes a stabilizing force. Even brief pauses before responding—just a moment to breathe and choose your words—can

> "Care is not erased by movement. It is revealed by how we adapt it."

shift the emotional tone of a digital conversation, whether in a group message, voice note, or livestream. People are drawn to presence, not perfection.

Digital Dignity and the Ethics of Visibility

And yet, not everything should be online. As the world turns to digital platforms for connection, crisis zones become dangerously visible. People share trauma without consent. They document distress as if it were content. However, visibility is not always justice. When pain becomes performance, dignity is lost. As a leader, you may need to intervene—not with force, but with gentle guidance. Remind others that not every moment is meant to be shared. Not every grief is meant to be recorded. There is wisdom in discretion and compassion in protecting the sacred.

This is especially important in communities already influenced by historical surveillance, exploitation, or media misuse. For instance, in Haiti, families were filmed grieving during cholera outbreaks—sometimes without understanding the purpose of the cameras. In South Africa, post-apartheid communities have faced digital scrutiny that reproduces old patterns of erasure. Visibility without context represents another form of erasure. When you engage online, consider what you're amplifying—and why.

Calm is Still the Strongest Signal

None of this means digital tools should be avoided. In fact, they can be lifelines. A clear voice note can reunite families. A well-timed update can de-escalate tension. A structured message thread can help organize food drops. The key is using these tools with emotional discipline: knowing when to post—and when not to; understanding how to interrupt panic without shutting down the truth; and allowing digital rhythms to follow emotional steadiness—not chaos.

In high-stakes moments, the most powerful thing you can offer may not be information, but calm. A tone that reassures. A pause that invites breath. A message that conveys, "We are thinking together. We are not alone. We are still here."

Leadership amidst the digital storm demands the same skills as leadership in the physical realm: presence, clarity, compassion, and care.

When noise fills the air, you become the signal.

Closing Insight: What Spreads, Sticks

In every crisis, words travel faster than water. A message whispered in panic can circle the globe before the truth catches up. But the same is true for clarity, steadiness, and calm.

You do not have to silence every rumor.

You only have to be one voice—clear, grounded, and consistent—when others are unsure who to trust.

In an age of digital noise, your leadership will be remembered not by how loudly you spoke, but by how wisely you communicated. Presence—online or off—is still the most reliable signal in the storm. Let your voice be one they follow—not because it's the most frequent, but because it's the most trusted.

Daily Anchor for Leading Anyway

Recovery is more than logistics — it is emotional work. I honor the invisible weight carried by those I serve and by myself. Healing requires patience, presence, and emotional steadiness. My leadership holds space for grief and growth to coexist. I allow recovery to unfold without forcing its pace.

> *Quietly or aloud, say after me:*
> **"I lead with emotional steadiness. I hold space for healing to emerge in its own time."**

🌐 CHAPTER 15 LEADERSHIP SNAPSHOT 🌐

 FRAMEWORK IN ACTION

This chapter centers on three vital pillars of the *Global Leadership Framework*:

Operational Clarity: By integrating emotional needs into recovery systems and logistics.

Emotional Centering: By affirming that recovery without emotional scaffolding is incomplete.

Cultural Coordination: By designing systems that respect emotional timelines and lived realities.

 KEY LEADERSHIP TAKEAWAYS

- ▷ Recovery is not just about infrastructure—it is about emotional scaffolding.
- ▷ Systems should be designed to affirm dignity, agency, and psychological safety.
- ▷ Emotional recovery must be planned for, resourced, and staffed—not left to chance.
- ▷ Checklists without care will eventually collapse under relational strain.

▶ The way a system "feels" determines whether people will return to it—or avoid it.

REFLECTIVE JOURNAL QUESTIONS

1 What emotions are our current systems affirming—or ignoring—in recovery?

2 How can we design for dignity, not just efficiency?

3 Am I asking: "What do people need emotionally to move forward?" as often as I ask "What do they need logistically?"

CULTURAL INSIGHT

Global models of recovery often emphasize speed and scale—but emotional recovery requires patience, presence, and cultural nuance. In some regions, spiritual healing, storytelling, or ancestral practices are central to restoration. Chapter 15 reminds us: systems that ignore culture and emotion may function on paper—but they fracture in practice.

USE THIS SECTION TO:

▶ Help NGOs, governments, and school systems audit their recovery protocols for emotional impact

▶ Integrate trauma-informed practices into every stage of disaster management

▶ Shift from reactive care to intentional emotional design in policies and practices

▶ Embed emotional literacy into all operational frameworks and team briefings

Chapter 16

Designing Recovery Spaces: Structure, Culture, and Emotional Safety

Spaces Convey Messages

Long after the shaking ceases and the waters recede, people remember how a space made them feel. Relief tents. School classrooms. Medical centers. Community kitchens. These environments become more than logistical zones—they transform into emotional containers. Following a crisis, the design of a space communicates just as power-

"Spiritual care does not require sameness— it requires reverence."

fully as any spoken message. Is this a place of safety or surveillance? Dignity or control? Compassion or chaos?

From Functional to Human-Centered

Too often, recovery spaces are viewed as purely functional: How many people can fit? How many supplies can we store? How quickly can this be assembled? However, trauma-informed leadership neces-sitates another question: how does this space feel to someone experiencing grief, fear, or disorientation? In shelters, clinics, and even make-shift classrooms, emotional safety is essential. Lighting, noise, seating, and signage—these are not luxuries; they are indicators. They inform the body whether it can settle or needs to remain alert.

Structure is a Kindness

In a time when people feel disoriented, structure becomes a form of care. Clear pathways. Visible signage. Predictable routines. These might seem small—but to someone who has lost their bearings, they create a sense of orientation.

In Port-au-Prince, following the 2010 earthquake, some of the most effective temporary clinics were not the biggest or most well-funded. They were the ones that established clear flows—quiet spaces for elders, child-friendly corners, and designated intake rhythms. Structure allowed presence to emerge.

Culture is the Atmosphere

However, structure alone isn't enough. Culture shapes how people behave within a space. Is this a place where everyone talks over one another, or is it a space where people are gently heard? Are volunteers treated as interchangeable labor, or are they seen as members of the community? Does the language on the wall reflect the diversity of those who enter, or is it represented only in one dialect? Recovery spaces need both order and atmosphere. The best ones radiate warmth, respect, and enough flexibility to respond to what arises. In addition to structure and culture, leaders must also honor the spiritual and ancestral threads that give communities meaning amidst displacement. This is where spiritual integrity becomes essential to designing recovery spaces.

The Role of Spiritual Integrity in Recovery

Disasters impact not only the physical world but also the inner lives of individuals—their sense of meaning, belonging, and identity. In these moments, spiritual leadership often rises quietly alongside logistical responses. While spiritual leadership may sometimes be rooted in organized religion, it can also manifest through ancestral wisdom, cultural rituals, shared music, storytelling, or silent presence.

In post-crisis communities worldwide, various spiritual traditions offer stabilizing rhythms that help individuals reorient after trauma:

- In Buddhist communities across Southeast Asia, daily chanting grounds support displaced families residing in temporary shelters.
- In Indigenous communities throughout the Americas, the retelling of creation stories and the practice of collective prayer circles serve to reconnect generations after natural disasters.
- In Islamic communities affected by floods in Pakistan, daily prayers, charitable giving (zakat), and mutual aid networks foster collective care.
- In faith-based Christian communities in certain parts of the Caribbean, singing hymns and coming together for shared meals serve as emotional anchors when physical homes are lost.
- In African villages impacted by drought, elders gather the youth to share ancestral resilience stories that have been transmitted orally for centuries.

These are not merely rituals; they act as stabilizing frameworks for emotional grounding. They remind individuals of their identity, even when everything else has transformed.

When you lead in these spaces, spiritual integrity requires sensitivity—honoring practices that preserve dignity without imposing your own beliefs. It means recognizing that for many, healing is as much about reconnecting with identity as it is about physical recovery.

"Faith won't replace planning—but it can anchor hope when everything else is uncertain."

You don't need to share the same beliefs to respect spiritual leadership; however, you must acknowledge its role as a subtle thread that helps communities rise again when everything else has fallen.

Designing for Inclusion, Not Just Efficiency

Often, in the rush to deliver, spaces are constructed quickly but with insufficient care. Accessibility is frequently overlooked. Neurodivergent needs are often neglected. Gender-neutral bathrooms are typically absent. Cultural rituals—such as spaces to pray, gather, or grieve—are frequently excluded. Inclusive design is not merely about being politically correct; it is fundamentally about being human. In Northern India, shelters that offered gender-segregated spaces saw a greater number of women return for ongoing aid. In Hawaii, outdoor recovery stations incorporated local flora and water rituals, which helped elders reconnect with ancestral memory. These are not extras; they are anchors.

> "You don't need to have all the answers to lead with soul."

Case Example
Arctic Evacuation in Northern Canada

In 2021, wildfires in Northern Canada forced several Indigenous communities to evacuate remote villages across the Yukon and Northwest Territories. Lacking adequate regional infrastructure, local tribal leaders coordinated community-wide airlifts, organized family group relocations, and ensured that familiar caregivers accompanied Elders during the journey. Cultural liaisons accompanied displaced residents to southern shelters, helping to maintain language, rituals, and spiritual practices throughout their prolonged displacement. Their leadership balanced cultural preservation with physical safety, protecting both the community's members and its identity under extreme duress.

Case Example
Syrian Refugee Leadership in Jordan

In the Zaatari refugee camp in Jordan, which houses tens of thousands displaced by the Syrian conflict, residents played a crucial role in creating safe spaces for families. Women's groups organized child-friendly areas where children could play and receive informal education. Religious leaders provided shared prayer spaces that offered emotional support for grieving families. Youth leaders organized soccer tournaments to channel stress into community engagement. While aid agencies supplied resources, it was the cultural leadership of the displaced individuals that transformed temporary shelters into emotionally protective environments.

Case Example
Flood Displacement in Nigeria

In 2022, extreme flooding displaced over 1.4 million people across Nigeria, with entire communities along the Niger and Benue Rivers forced into temporary camps. In the absence of adequate government shelters, many communities mobilized quickly. Local imams opened mosques as safe zones. Women's cooperatives managed food distribution, while volunteer teachers established makeshift classrooms under tarps and trees to restore a sense of normalcy for displaced children. Despite limited resources, these local leaders provided emotional support amid overwhelming uncertainty, stabilizing thousands long before outside agencies could scale formal response efforts.

Case Example
Youth Response Teams in Morocco

When a 6.8-magnitude earthquake struck Morocco's Atlas region, teen volunteers in small villages organized walking brigades to check on elders, deliver supplies, and document missing family members. They were not trained responders, but they moved with empathy, speed, and cultural clarity. In many cases, they were the first to arrive—and the last to leave.

When recovery spaces are designed solely for efficiency without considering emotional safety, the long-term impact can quietly unravel the very communities they seek to support. We often highlight best practices; however, equally important are the cautionary tales that show what occurs when care, culture, and community voice are excluded from the design process.

Case Example
L'Aquila, Italy (2009 Earthquake)

After the earthquake struck L'Aquila in 2009, the physical rebuild progressed rapidly. However, most decisions were made by centralized authorities without involving the local community. Homes and public spaces were reconstructed without considering how people had lived, gathered, or worked before the disaster. Over time, the disconnect between the new infrastructure and the community's cultural rhythms led to significant frustration. Social trust diminished. Many residents expressed feeling displaced even after returning home. The emotional cost: a hollow recovery, rich in concrete but poor in connection.

Case Example
Sulawesi, Indonesia (Post-2004 Tsunami Preparedness Breakdown)

After the 2004 tsunami, Indonesia invested in warning systems and community preparedness. However, by 2018, many systems were in disrepair, and communities were no longer engaged in emergency drills. When another tsunami struck Sulawesi, the warnings failed, leaving communities confused and unprotected. The lack of sustained trauma-informed training and visible memorialization meant that past pain was not transformed into readiness. The result was collective shock, a return to helplessness, and long-term distrust in public safety measures.

Case Example
New Orleans, USA (Post-Katrina Displacement and Emotional Recovery)

Hurricane Katrina's aftermath prompted extensive investment in infrastructure. Levees were reinforced, roads were repaired, and housing was gradually rebuilt. Yet community spaces—the emotional infrastructure of neighborhoods—remained overlooked. The absence of inclusive planning left many residents feeling voiceless. Mental health support was minimal at best. In the years that followed, rates of PTSD, substance use, and chronic illness soared. Without shared spaces for grief, storytelling, or remembrance, collective healing struggled to take root.

Recovery Without Emotional Anchors Is Not Recovery

These stories remind us that when emotional safety, culture, and inclusion are omitted from recovery planning, physical structures may rise, but the community spirit often does not. Designing recovery spaces involves not only functionality; it encompasses the restoration of meaning, memory, and connection.

The Role of the Leader in the Room

You do not need to be the architect to influence a space. In any cultural setting—whether under a tent, in a church hall, a school courtyard, or a community center—your presence shapes the emotional tone. As a leader, your voice sets the rhythm. Your pauses provide permission for others to exhale. A simple gesture of greeting—offered with respect, in any language or custom—can completely shift the atmosphere.

You can make meaningful requests: dim harsh lights, open windows to let in fresh air, play calming music, or invite silence, and arrange seating in a circle to promote connection. In some settings, this could mean placing mats on the floor instead of chairs or inviting elders to sit first. Each decision contributes to transforming the space—from a zone of transaction or urgency into one of dignity and care.

Maintaining the Space is Part of the Work

Over time, even the most thoughtfully designed environment can fray. Tensions rise. Supplies run low. Cleanliness slips. Culture shifts. A true leader notices, walks the room, reorients the tone, invites feedback, and delegates maintenance not just as a task—but as an act of shared care. When people help tend to the space, they invest emotionally. They begin to feel it is theirs. And what people feel ownership of, they are more likely to protect.

2021 Snapshot: The River That Rose (Brazil, Amazon Flooding)

In 2021, Brazil's Amazon region faced record-breaking floods as weeks of heavy rainfall swelled rivers far beyond their natural boundaries. Entire communities built along the waterways were swallowed overnight, with homes submerged, crops destroyed, and livelihoods washed away. In the heart of these flooded villages, leadership emerged from the community itself. Teachers became organizers, transforming schoolhouses into temporary shelters. Village elders coordinated boat rescues using hand-built canoes, ferrying stranded families to higher ground.

Faith leaders provided calm amid fear, gathering residents to pray, sing, and comfort anxious children while waters continued to rise. With outside aid delayed by damaged roads and logistical challenges, these local leaders maintained emotional steadiness, distributed scarce food supplies, and preserved the social fabric of their communities when the waters refused to recede. Long after the media moved on, their leadership continued quietly, helping neighbors rebuild homes, replant crops, and restore fragile hope along the riverbanks they had called home for generations.

Closing Insight: Designing the Invisible

Ultimately, the most powerful aspect of a recovery space is often what is not seen: a gesture of welcome, a safe place to cry, a quiet bench where someone can sit without being asked questions. These invisible features linger in memory long after the material assistance has faded. They are not found in the blueprints or measured by efficiency reports, but they shape how a person remembers their first sense of safety after chaos.

What makes a space sacred is rarely the structure alone; it is the energy, the softness, and the permission to be fully human within it. It is the feeling of being unjudged while grieving and of being witnessed without the pressure to perform recovery. These are the details that leaders, designers, and coordinators must hold with great care. While logistics can solve problems, it is these invisible gestures that offer dignity.

When we prioritize emotional safety alongside physical safety, we transform the entire recovery experience. We remind individuals that healing is not a process to rush, and survival does not signify the end of vulnerability. Therefore, we design with silence in mind, with grief in mind, and with moments of beauty, stillness, and grace intentionally incorporated into the environment.

That is what makes a space unforgettable—not just because it helped people survive, but because it quietly helped them feel human again.

▶ *Related Toolkit: Recovery Design Checklist (Do vs. Don't) (Appendix L)*

Daily Anchor for Leading Anyway

Displacement disrupts identity and belonging. I recognize the quiet losses hidden beneath physical relocation. My leadership becomes an anchor for those who have lost familiar ground. I offer stability, dignity, and compassion while helping others rebuild both externally and internally.

Quietly or aloud, say after me:
"I lead with compassion. I create safety and dignity for those who have lost their footing."

🌐 CHAPTER 16 LEADERSHIP SNAPSHOT 🌐

FRAMEWORK IN ACTION

This chapter draws on three foundational pillars of the *Global Leadership Framework*:

Cultural Coordination: By acknowledging place-based identity, loss, and belonging in global contexts.

Emotional Centering: By addressing the invisible grief and disorientation that accompanies displacement.

Collective Power and Voice: By creating leadership practices that preserve dignity and voice in temporary spaces.

KEY LEADERSHIP TAKEAWAYS

- Displacement is not just logistical—it is deeply emotional and cultural.
- The loss of home also means the loss of routine, rhythm, safety, and self-definition.
- Leading displaced communities requires trauma-aware, identity-sensitive communication.
- Restoring agency begins with restoring voice—inviting people to name what matters to them now.
- Temporary environments must still offer consistency, compassion, and cultural respect.

REFLECTIVE JOURNAL QUESTIONS

1. How do I support a sense of identity and dignity in transitional or temporary spaces?

2. What systems can we create that reduce emotional chaos during displacement?

3. Am I listening for emotional loss—not just physical needs?

CULTURAL INSIGHT

In many cultures, land and place are tied to ancestry, memory, and spiritual grounding. Displacement interrupts more than housing—it interrupts identity. Chapter 16 urges leaders to see displacement not as a stopgap issue, but as a core leadership challenge that demands cultural sensitivity, emotional wisdom, and humanizing strategy.

USE THIS SECTION TO:

▶ Train shelter managers, educators, and emergency teams in emotional regulation within high-mobility settings
▶ Design culturally respectful intake and relocation procedures
▶ Help leaders recognize loss of routine as a core trauma trigger
▶ Build temporary systems that feel humane, inclusive, and predictable

Chapter 17

The Spirit of Response

The Quiet Path to Clarity: Leading Yourself Through Emotional Overload

When the Fog Is Inside You

There comes a point in disaster response when the external chaos begins to quiet—but the internal noise only grows louder. You've made decisions, held steady, and kept others calm. Yet suddenly, your own clarity feels dim. You forget things, doubt yourself, replay moments, and feel unmoored even in calm weather. This is not failure; it is the delayed echo of everything you've carried.

You Can Be Steady and Still Struggling

Leadership does not mean immunity. You can be emotionally intelligent, culturally aware, and deeply present—and still feel overwhelmed. Emotional overload doesn't always appear dramatic. Sometimes it manifests as numbness, the inability to answer a simple question,

> "Legacy leadership begins where ego ends—at the intersection of service, humility, and shared humanity."

or an urge to stay busy just to avoid stillness. The work you've done may be invisible to others, but your nervous system remembers it, and eventually, it demands rest.

Clarity Requires Space, Not Just Strategy

Most leaders try to "push through"—to read more, plan better, and delegate more effectively. But clarity doesn't come from just more effort. It arises from creating space—emotionally, mentally, and even physically. This might mean a morning without meetings, a walk without your phone, or a conversation where you're not the one offering guidance. Space doesn't delay leadership; it strengthens it.

You Don't Have to Prove You're Okay

In many systems—especially in high-performance or high-pressure cultures—there is strong pressure to recover and resume normal functioning as quickly as possible. To lead without showing any signs of struggle. However, post-crisis leadership requires inner congruence. People trust you not just because you sound strong, but because they sense when your inner and outer states align. Acknowledging your own overwhelm—in healthy, contained ways—models honesty. And honesty builds trust faster than perfection ever could.

Presence Doesn't Mean Performance

You can lead a debrief while being quiet. You can sit beside someone in silence. You can say "I don't have words today" and still lead. Emotional presence is not about being expressive. It is about being anchored. Others feel it. When you are honest about your own limitations, you invite others to stop pretending too. That shared humanity becomes the foundation for renewed connection.

A Moment Can Reset Everything

You don't need a week off to reconnect with yourself. Sometimes, it takes just a breath. A question posed by someone who doesn't expect you to fix anything. A memory that brings you back to purpose. A stillness that reminds you that your worth lies not in what you solve—but in who you are while solving it. These resets aren't indulgent. They are essential.

> "After the storm, what remains is not just what you rebuilt, but how you made people feel seen in the rubble."

Let Others Hold You, Too

The strongest leaders know when to be held, when to call the person who sees through their armor, when to sit in a room and not speak, and when to cry, sleep, laugh, or pray. You were never meant to bear the entire weight of a community alone. Let someone hold part of you, too. That vulnerability will not break you—it will ground you. In doing so, it will return you to the clarity you've been seeking.

Case Example
The Prayer Circle in Mindanao (Philippines)

After an earthquake displaced thousands in Mindanao, a local teacher gathered both Christian and Muslim students in a circle each evening. No doctrine—just gratitude, quiet prayer, and shared silence. The ritual provided emotional regulation across faiths. The teacher later said, "We didn't know what would happen next, but we knew we'd face it together." That circle—multigenerational, interfaith, and steady—became the emotional anchor for hundreds.

Case Example
Floating Kindness in Aceh, Indonesia

Following the 2004 tsunami, survivors in Aceh began floating hand-carved wooden hearts down flooded streets. Each one bore a hand-written message—"We're still here," "You are not alone," "Our hearts survived." What began as a gesture of grief became a citywide ritual of connection and remembrance.

Case Example
A Radio Voice in Maiduguri, Nigeria

During violent insurgency and displacement, a former teacher in Maiduguri began hosting nightly radio broadcasts focused on calm breathing, poetry, and children's bedtime stories. The program became a vital emotional tether for families in camps, rebuilding a sense of normalcy and safety through sound.

Case Example
The Rooftop Quiet in Kabul, Afghanistan

After a bombing shook parts of Kabul, an elder began holding rooftop tea gatherings—no discussion, just silence and steam rising into the air. These rooftop moments became a space for collective breath. In the quiet, people remembered their humanity and their hope.

Closing Insight: What the World Still Needs

In the end, the spirit of response is not defined by credentials, titles, or even certainty. It is defined by your willingness to remain present when things fall apart—and to return, again and again, to the quiet space where clarity is reborn. The world will need you tomorrow, not just as a responder, but as a whole human. A steady voice. A willing presence. A living example of what it means to lead, even when no one is watching.

> "When systems are slow and hearts are broken, it is the spirit of the response that carries people forward."

Daily Anchor for Leading Anyway

The way I lead matters as much as what I do. I carry the spirit of service, humility, and courage into every response. My leadership is not transactional — it is human. In every decision, I choose to lead with integrity that honors both the moment and the people within it.

> *Quietly or aloud, say after me:*
> **"I lead with integrity and heart. My leadership serves both the moment and the person."**

🌐 CHAPTER 17 LEADERSHIP SNAPSHOT 🌐

 FRAMEWORK IN ACTION

This chapter weaves together all elements of the *Global Leadership Framework* and especially emphasizes:

Emotional Centering: By reminding leaders that how we respond is as important as what we do.

Cultural Coordination: By honoring the unseen, unmeasurable aspects of collective care and healing.

Collective Power and Voice: By celebrating the moral clarity and spiritual steadiness that undergird human-centered leadership.

KEY LEADERSHIP TAKEAWAYS

▷ Crisis leadership is not just about coordination—it is about presence, tone, and intention.

▷ The most powerful responses are often quiet, unseen, and emotionally attuned.

▷ Cultural rituals, shared songs, and communal gestures restore coherence during chaos.

▷ Responding with humanity means choosing care over compliance when they conflict.

▷ The spirit behind your leadership will linger longer than any operational checklist.

REFLECTIVE JOURNAL QUESTIONS

1. What spirit am I bringing into the room before I speak or act?

2. Do our systems reflect compassion—or just control?

3. What part of this work feels sacred to me—and how am I protecting that?

CULTURAL INSIGHT

Around the world, disaster response is often rooted in spiritual practice—from prayers said before meals in shelters to collective mourning rituals. Chapter 17 invites leaders to lead with heart, humility, and reverence—not just for outcomes, but for the humanity unfolding in real time.

USE THIS SECTION TO:

- Teach leaders to attune to emotional atmospheres, not just agendas
- Design responses that affirm dignity, identity, and interconnectedness
- Recenter the values of care, patience, and presence in operational spaces
- Encourage culturally grounded practices that help communities grieve, regroup, and move forward

A Message to the Global Leader Reading This

You held this book not just in your hands—but in your heart.
You turned these pages not for theory, but for strength.
And somewhere, between the lines, you saw yourself.

You are the leader who does not wait for a title.
The one who steps forward when others freeze.
Who holds the tension between care and clarity,
between grief and grace,
between chaos and calm.

This work is not easy.
To lead in crisis is to love deeply while navigating danger.
It is to speak when the words are caught in your throat.
To stay when it would be easier to leave.
To listen when you are already carrying too much.
And yet—you do it anyway.

You do it in refugee camps and crowded classrooms.
In overstretched clinics and policy war rooms.
In rural villages and broken cities.
You do it in languages not your own,
in places not always safe,
in systems that often forget the human soul.

And still—you lead.

This is your reminder:
You were never asked to do this alone.
You are not the source of all hope—but you are a vessel of it.
You are not perfect—but you are present.
And that presence matters more than you know.

Let this be your grounding:
You are allowed to rest.
You are allowed to feel.
You are allowed to not know the next step.
But when you rise—and you will rise—
do so with gentleness for yourself
and resolve for the world you're helping rebuild.

Because leadership is not about having all the answers.
It is about standing in the storm,
hands steady, heart open,
and saying: "We will find the way. Together."

You are that kind of leader.
And the world is better for it.

Epilogue: You Led Through the Fire

There is no handbook that fully prepares you for this kind of leadership. There are no perfect credentials, no linear path, and no guarantee of applause. There is only a moment that calls your name—and the quiet courage to say yes, even when part of you hopes someone else might step forward first. And yet, you answered.

You did not simply respond to a crisis; you steadied others through it. You showed up in moments of chaos, stood firm in uncertainty, and chose to lead with presence. You felt fear, yet moved forward anyway. You held space for grief, confusion, and anger—often while managing your own. You led not because it was easy, but because it was necessary.

This type of leadership rarely makes headlines. It often goes unnoticed by those too far removed to witness what you held together. But those nearby—the people whose voices you listened to, whose hands you steadied, whose fears you helped calm—they will remember. They may forget the specific plans or protocols, but they will remember how you made them feel when everything else was breaking: safer, seen, and supported.

That is the essence of crisis leadership: not control, not perfection, but presence.

You led through the fire.

Disaster leadership is no longer limited by borders, titles, or institutional roles. It belongs to those who choose to remain steady in the face of fear—across languages, cultures, and geographies. This book reflects only a portion of the global leadership I continue to witness and contribute to. May it serve those who step forward quietly—carrying both the weight and the healing long after the cameras have disappeared.

And for many others, although not physically present, the images that reached their screens still touched their hearts. They, too, carried silent weight—witnessing grief from afar and holding space for suffering that transcended time zones and national borders. Presence matters, even from a distance.

You might be a school administrator who kept your staff grounded, a village elder who offered shelter and guidance, a nurse who stayed past your shift, or a youth leader who transformed fear into coordination. You may have created spaces that comforted others, sent messages that calmed fears, or quietly stepped back when the fog within you needed clearing. You might not have had all the answers. You could have doubted yourself more times than you can count. You may still carry the weight of what was lost. And yet—you showed up. Fully human. Fully willing. And that matters more than you realize.

As the world continues to face waves of uncertainty—through storms, displacement, global emergencies, and structural breakdowns—leaders like you will be needed time and time again. Not necessarily those with the loudest voices or the most polished résumés, but those with the emotional integrity to remain steady, the humility to listen, and the quiet courage to put people before process.

And now, you have done more than survive. You have created rhythms of care. You have chosen clarity over performance. You have built spaces that restore. You have spoken when words were hard to find, and you remained present when words were not enough.

This kind of leadership does not fade over time—it expands. It ripples outward into classrooms and community centers, into boardrooms and homes, into relief tents and quiet conversations. It endures in the way others lead after you—because of you.

You may never receive formal recognition. You may never fully share what you endured. But know this: your presence made recovery possible.

So take a breath. And when you are ready, look in the mirror—not with fatigue, but with clarity. You did not just survive the storm. You led through it. And that kind of leadership—the kind rooted in presence, compassion, wisdom, and resilience—will always be needed.

Especially in the silence that follows.

Especially in the storm that returns.

Especially in you.

Standing at Ground Zero Years Later

The memorial was quiet that morning. The early sun reflected off the smooth black stone, with water gently cascading into the hollow where the towers once stood. Names etched in granite wrapped around the perimeter—each representing a life, each telling a story. Tourists walked slowly, some pausing to trace the engraved letters with their fingertips, while others stood silently, eyes closed and heads bowed.

I stood there too. Years had passed since that morning when I first watched the towers fall from my college campus, paralyzed in disbelief. I had long graduated, built a career, and stepped into leadership roles of my own. But standing here now, I felt the weight of those early moments all over again.

The buildings were gone, but the story remained. The loss was permanent, yet the life that continued afterward was undeniable. The city had rebuilt, and people had carried on. The survivors had found ways to move forward while still holding space for what had been lost.

As I stood there, I did not see a memorial to destruction. I saw a reflection of what leadership truly becomes after disaster: not the absence of loss, but the presence of resolve. The decision to rebuild when there are no guarantees. The courage to lead when there are no perfect answers. The discipline to stand steady even when memories still tremble beneath your feet.

We do not always choose the storms we encounter. But we can choose how we lead after they pass.

Glossary of Key Terms

Aftershock (Emotional): The psychological and emotional responses that surface after the immediate danger of a disaster has passed, often expressed as fatigue, irritability, grief, or withdrawal.

Aid Fatigue: The emotional, financial, or organizational exhaustion experienced by donors, agencies, responders, or communities after prolonged or recurring crises with limited resolution or recovery progress.

Collective Trauma: The shared psychological impact experienced by communities as a result of disasters, violence, or historical oppression, often influencing identity, behavior, and resilience across generations.

Community Intelligence: The lived knowledge, relational trust, and informal networks held by local leaders that allow communities to adapt and respond to crisis more quickly than external systems.

Compassion Fatigue: A state of emotional and physical exhaustion that can affect individuals who are repeatedly exposed to others' trauma and distress.

Crisis Leadership: The act of guiding others through uncertainty and instability with clarity, presence, and emotional resilience—often without formal authority.

Cross-Cultural Negotiation: The skill of facilitating agreements between partners with differing cultural norms, leadership structures, and decision-making styles, requiring flexibility, emotional intelligence, and shared purpose.

Cultural Competence: The ability to understand, honor, and adapt to the cultural contexts of communities being served, especially during times of crisis.

Cultural Coordination (Framework Layer): The leadership practice of partnering with local elders, grassroots leaders, cultural anchors, and community knowledge holders to design services that honor cultural, spiritual, and relational realities.

Cultural Humility: A leadership stance that acknowledges the limits of one's own cultural understanding, remaining open, teachable, and respectful of local traditions, hierarchies, and histories while leading in cross-cultural environments.

Digital Trauma: The emotional and physiological stress response experienced when individuals are repeatedly exposed to images, stories, or live footage of disasters, violence, or crises through digital platforms, even if they are not physically present. Digital trauma silently accumulates, negatively impacting mental health, emotional regulation, and leadership capacity in an age of constant global visibility.

Displacement: The condition of individuals or communities being forced to leave their homes due to conflict, disaster, or environmental disruption, often resulting in trauma and disrupted social support systems.

Donor Dependency: A long-term risk in disaster recovery where communities become reliant on external funding, undermining local ownership, resilience, and sustainable rebuilding.

Emotional Centering (Framework Layer): The foundational leadership skill of regulating your own nervous system, recognizing emotional aftershock, and grounding yourself before leading others.

Emotional Debris: The lingering emotional impact of a disaster that can manifest as stress, anxiety, fear, or hopelessness.

Emotional Regulation: The skill of managing your own nervous system and emotional state in high-stress environments in order to respond calmly and effectively.

Emergency Coordination: The strategic process of aligning people, resources, and systems during a disaster response to ensure efficient action and reduce duplication or harm.

Equity Lens: A leadership practice that evaluates whether power, resources, decision-making, and recovery opportunities are being distributed fairly across diverse populations, especially in the aftermath of crisis.

Field Coordination: The process of organizing people, resources, and information on the ground during disaster response to reduce confusion and enhance impact.

Grounding: A practice used to help individuals reconnect with the present moment and stabilize their nervous system during stress.

Hope as a Skill: The intentional, practiced choice to believe in the possibility of recovery and progress, even when the outcome is uncertain.

Human Infrastructure: The web of relationships, emotional safety, and communication practices that form the backbone of community resilience.

Inclusive Communication: A form of messaging that is sensitive to cultural, emotional, and linguistic differences and centers dignity and trust.

Informal Leadership: Authority and influence held by individuals without formal titles, who are trusted by the community and often step into leadership roles during crisis.

Local Leadership: Individuals from within the affected community—such as elders, teachers, youth, or faith leaders—who provide trusted, culturally grounded guidance.

Long-Term Meaning and Recovery (Framework Layer): The leadership outcome of fostering emotional safety, preserving identity, and building local capacity for sustainable healing after the initial crisis period.

Moral Injury: The internal distress that occurs when a person feels forced to act (or is unable to act) in ways that contradict their values during a crisis.

Operational Calm: The state of maintaining logistical clarity and emotional regulation in leadership roles, particularly in high-stress field environments.

Parallel Leadership Structures: Situations where external agencies and local leadership operate simultaneously in the same recovery effort, requiring intentional alignment of authority, trust, and communication pathways to avoid confusion and fragmentation.

Polyvagal Theory: A neuroscience framework that explains how the body's autonomic nervous system responds to stress, fear, and safety, directly influencing emotional regulation and leadership presence in high-stress situations.

Post-Crisis Meaning-Making: The emotional and cognitive process of integrating what happened during a disaster and exploring what it means for identity, relationships, and future direction.

Presence (Framework Layer): The leadership act of showing up with full emotional steadiness, physical calm, and attentiveness, creating psychological safety even in uncertain situations.

Psychological First Aid (PFA): A framework used in disaster response that prioritizes establishing safety, restoring calm, and connecting individuals to emotional and physical resources.

Psychosocial Support: Services and informal support systems that address the emotional, psychological, and social well-being of individuals affected by crisis.

Recovery Fatigue: The exhaustion that sets in after long-term crisis involvement, often felt by both communities and responders as they try to maintain momentum and hope.

Recovery Ownership: The transfer of responsibility, leadership, and decision-making back to local leaders and communities as external responders transition out, ensuring sustainable, culturally grounded long-term recovery.

Reset Routine: A short, structured series of actions to regulate emotions and support mental clarity, especially in leadership roles.

Resilience: The capacity of individuals, communities, and systems to recover from adversity and rebuild stronger, emotionally and structurally.

Social Infrastructure: The informal and formal relationships, networks, and institutions that support emotional and community stability in the face of disruption.

Soft Power Dynamics: The unspoken influence that cultural norms, historical relationships, or external actors may exert over local leadership and decision-making during disaster recovery or international partnerships.

Trauma-Informed Leadership: An approach that considers how past trauma affects behavior and decision-making, and centers emotional safety and relational trust.

Trust Anchor: A person or practice that community members look to for safety, guidance, and stability in the midst of disruption.

Trust Capital: The reserve of credibility, relational integrity, and goodwill that leaders build over time and draw upon in moments of crisis.

Village Leadership (or Grassroots Leadership): Non-formal leadership that arises from within the community and is rooted in relational trust, local knowledge, and lived experience.

Appendices

Supporting Your Leadership After the Storm

The appendices that follow are designed to serve as practical tools and reflection anchors for leaders navigating disaster recovery, emotional fatigue, and collective care. These resources are not academic extras—they are extensions of the book's mission to ground leadership in presence, clarity, and cultural humility.

Each appendix offers a different layer of support—from quick-reference checklists and recovery exercises to global case studies and facilitation guides. Use what serves you now, revisit what may serve you later, and adapt these tools to meet the evolving needs of your context.

Leadership in the wake of disaster is rarely linear. Let these appendices be a companion—not a prescription—as you find your own way forward.

Appendix A

Crisis Communication Toolkit

Phrases + Tone Guidelines for High-Stress Situations

When emotions run high, words carry amplified weight. These grounding phrases and tone guidelines are designed to help leaders and responders communicate with steadiness, compassion, and clarity.

Grounding Phrases

- "Here's what we know right now."
- "I'm here with you. We're going to take this step by step."
- "It's okay to feel overwhelmed. You're not alone."
- "Let's pause and breathe before we decide."

Tone Guidelines

- Speak slowly and clearly—speed communicates panic.
- Use a steady, grounded voice, even if you feel uncertain.
- Avoid making promises; offer reassurance without false certainty.
- When possible, ask before directing: "Would it help if we...?"

Appendix B

5-Minute Reset Routines for Teams and Leaders

Rapid Emotional Regulation Tools

Emotional recovery doesn't require hours. These short, structured practices support nervous system regulation and team stability before, during, or after stressful events.

Solo Reset (Leader Use)

1. Step away for 90 seconds—physical space supports mental clarity.
2. Practice 4-2-6 breathing (inhale 4, hold 2, exhale 6) for three cycles.
3. Ground by pressing feet into the floor; name three physical sensations.
4. Affirm quietly: "I can respond with clarity."

Group Reset (Team Use)

1. Regroup in silence for 30 seconds to establish presence.
2. Lead with: "Let's all take one deep breath together."
3. Offer a grounding phrase: "We're here to support, not to perfect."
4. Name the next small, manageable task with clarity.

Appendix C

Cultural Checklists for Global Use

Building Respectful, Inclusive Crisis Responses

Use these prompts as conversation openers—not assumptions—when engaging diverse communities during disaster response and recovery.

Ask:

- How is trust typically established here?
- Who are the informal influencers or decision-makers?
- Are direct questions embraced or avoided?
- What roles do elders, youth, or spiritual leaders play?
- Are there any gestures, words, or behaviors that may unintentionally offend?

Observe:

- Unspoken hierarchies (age, gender, class, education, language)
- Differences in body language (eye contact, proximity, gestures)
- Local customs related to grief, caregiving, and communal gatherings

Appendix D

Age-Specific Support Quick Guide

Tailoring Emotional Support Across Generations

Children

- Use clear, simple language.
- Offer predictable, temporary routines.
- Reassure them gently—without overpromising.
- Allow space for play, drawing, or quiet presence.

Teens

- Involve them in meaningful, age-appropriate roles.
- Validate their emotional experience without minimizing.
- Respect their need for autonomy while maintaining structure.

Elders

- Speak slowly and allow processing time.
- Respect memory, vision, or mobility limitations without condescension.
- Invite their wisdom into decision-making, not just caregiving plans.

Appendix E

Field Templates

For Use in Briefings, Journals, and Low-Tech Settings

Daily Leadership Log Template

Date:

Top 3 Priorities Today

_____
_____
_____

Team Check-In Notes

_____
_____
_____

Key Communications Shared

_____
_____
_____

Emotional Tone Observed

_____

_____

_____

Personal Reset Completed?   □ Yes   □ No

Follow-Up Needed Tomorrow

_____

_____

_____

Coordination Sheet (Team Briefing Use)

Location/Zone

_____

_____

_____

Supplies In/Out

_____

_____

_____

Assigned Roles

_____

_____

_____

Risks or Safety Concerns Identified

_____

_____

_____

Support Requests Sent

_____

_____

_____

Additional Notes

_____

_____

_____

Templates can be printed or adapted for
digital or no-tech environments.

Appendix F

Certificate of Completion

For Internal Use in Training and Leadership Development Settings

---

CERTIFICATE OF COMPLETION

This certifies that

[Name]

has completed training in
Emotionally Intelligent Leadership in Crisis and Disaster Recovery based on the book
Leading After the Storm: How to Communicate, Calm, and Coordinate in the Wake of Disaster

by Dr. Karissa Thomas   Date: _____

Trainer Signature: _____

This certificate may be used for internal recognition or professional development. It is not a credential or licensure.

Appendix G

Global Field Leadership Reflection Guide

These questions aim to assist local leaders, trainers, and field responders in reflecting on their leadership practices when serving communities during and after a crisis. They can be utilized in workshops, certification programs, NGO training sessions, university courses, or personal development.

1. Emotional Regulation
When a crisis arises, how reliably can I steady my own emotions before guiding others?
Where do I need to improve my personal reset practices?

2. Presence and Communication
Am I fostering a tone of calm, clarity, and dignity when I speak?
Do those I lead feel emotionally safe when I communicate under pressure?

3. Cultural Awareness
How well do I understand the cultural, spiritual, and historical context of the community I serve? Have I taken the time to listen and observe before offering solutions?

4. Trust and Community Intelligence
Who possesses natural leadership and relational trust within the community?
Am I including their wisdom in the decision-making processes?

5. Coordination and Delegation

Am I aligning tasks with individuals' energy, skills, and emotional capacity?

Am I providing opportunities for others to contribute meaningfully without overwhelming them?

6. Advocacy and Boundaries

When external organizations arrive, can I effectively advocate for what the community truly needs?

Am I upholding local dignity while also fostering beneficial partnerships?

7. Age-Specific Care

Am I aware of the distinct emotional needs of children, elders, and multigenerational families?

Am I creating spaces and routines that allow each group to feel safe and acknowledged?

8. Inclusion and Equity

Who could be unintentionally left out of the recovery process?

How can I ensure that marginalized voices have a space in planning and decision-making?

9. Self-Care and Sustainability

Am I establishing a leadership rhythm that promotes rest, reflection, and personal care?

Am I demonstrating sustainable leadership for those who follow my example?

10. Long-Term Meaning and Recovery

Am I helping the community not only to rebuild structures but also to restore identity, meaning, and belonging?

What legacy am I contributing to as this recovery continues?

How to Use This Guide:

These questions can be revisited individually or discussed in teams. They can be utilized during training seminars, leadership retreats, NGO onboarding sessions, or post-crisis debriefs to promote ongoing reflection and growth.

Appendix H

Daily Anchors for Leading Anyway

This section compiles all the Daily Anchors from each chapter into one location. As you revisit these anchors, you can express them aloud, reflect on them quietly, or utilize them as grounding reminders during leadership moments that call for clarity and steadiness.

Chapter 1 – When the Ground Shakes Inside You

As I step forward from this chapter, I recognize that leadership often begins in the quiet tremors inside my own soul. The world may shift, but I do not have to collapse with it. My steadiness is not the absence of fear, but the choice to remain rooted even as everything moves around me. Each moment of uncertainty becomes an opportunity to strengthen the ground beneath my own feet.
"Even when the ground shakes, I stand. My stability is not dependent on my circumstances. I am steady. I am grounded."

Chapter 2 – The Power of Calm Leadership

I release the need to react. I allow calm to rise inside me, even when others are overcome by emotion or urgency. My calm leadership is not passive — it is my power. I create space for clarity to emerge, for thoughtful decisions to unfold, and for others to find steadiness in my presence. This is the leadership I choose to embody.

"I lead with calm. My presence sets the tone. My peace makes room for solutions."

Chapter 3 – Leading in the Fog

I accept that not every step will be clear. The fog does not mean I am lost. I move forward with what I know, trusting that clarity will meet me along the way. Leadership in the fog is not about waiting for perfect conditions; it is about the courage to keep walking with grace, wisdom, and patience.

"I trust the process even when the path is unclear. I move forward with courage, knowing the fog will lift."

Chapter 4 – Speak So They Can Hear You

My words are a tool of leadership. I release the need to force or demand. Instead, I choose language that opens hearts, clarifies intentions, and allows truth to land where it is needed. I honor both the message and the moment. When I speak, I am not only heard — I am understood.

"I speak with clarity, respect, and wisdom. My words create understanding and open doors."

Chapter 5 – Step Forward Anyway

Leadership requires motion. Even when uncertainty whispers and fear tries to stall my progress, I choose forward movement. Courage is not the absence of hesitation — it is the decision to keep stepping through it. I give myself permission to act without waiting for perfect readiness. My leadership grows with each step I take.

"I step forward with courage. Progress is made one decision at a time. I am in motion."

Chapter 6 – Organizing the Chaos

I do not fear the mess. Chaos is simply unorganized opportunity. I bring order by calming my mind, clarifying my priorities, and guiding others

toward steady ground. My leadership creates rhythm where there was once disorder. I am equipped to bring structure to complexity.
"I bring order to complexity. I see the pieces clearly. I lead through chaos with calm authority."

Chapter 7 – When the System Isn't Ready

Systems may fail, but my leadership does not have to collapse with them. I release my frustration over what others have not prepared, and I focus on what I can create within the moment I am given. I become the stability that others need, even when the system lags behind. My leadership fills the gaps with wisdom, flexibility, and compassion.
"I rise even when the system stumbles. My leadership adapts, steadies, and carries forward."

Chapter 8 – Age-Specific Care

Every person I serve carries unique needs, shaped by age, stage, and experience. I meet each individual where they are, adjusting my approach with care, wisdom, and emotional understanding. My leadership honors both the child and the elder, the dependent and the caregiver. I lead with sensitivity, not assumption.
"I lead with discernment. I see the person in front of me and respond with wisdom and care."

Chapter 9 – Coordinating with Outside Help

True leadership does not fear collaboration. I recognize that I am not called to carry everything alone. By coordinating with others, I expand the strength of what can be accomplished. My leadership is not diminished by partnership — it is multiplied through shared expertise, trust, and humility.
"I lead with openness. Collaboration strengthens my leadership. Together, we accomplish more."

Chapter 10 – Crisis Within the Crisis

Even when new storms emerge inside the existing ones, I remain anchored. I acknowledge the weight of compounded challenges without surrendering to them. My leadership holds steady as I tend to the urgent while preserving long-term stability. I am present, composed, and capable, even when layers of crisis press in.

"I remain steady within the layers. My leadership does not fracture under pressure. I navigate complexity with calm strength."

Chapter 11 – The Digital Storm

I do not confuse my care with my capacity. My heart remains open, but my gate remains guarded. I feel without drowning. I serve without collapsing. I am emotionally available for what I am called to hold, and I release what does not belong to me.

"I guard my emotional gate. I carry what is mine and release what is not. My peace protects my leadership."

Chapter 12 – The Leader's Survival Plan

My leadership requires care for both others and myself. I am not immune to depletion, and I refuse to sacrifice my own well-being in the name of performance. I build rhythms that sustain me. I preserve my capacity to serve by honoring rest, reflection, and recalibration as non-negotiable parts of my leadership.

"I protect my capacity. My leadership is strengthened by care, rhythm, and intentional restoration."

Chapter 13 – Beyond the Storm

Storms do not define me. I acknowledge what I've endured, but I refuse to live anchored to the past. My leadership is not rooted in survival alone, but in renewal. I step forward carrying wisdom, not wounds. Beyond the storm, I build with clarity, gratitude, and quiet strength.

"I am not what I survived. I lead from wisdom, not from wounds. The future is open before me."

Chapter 14 – Hope Is a Skill

Hope is not something I wait to feel. It is a discipline I choose to practice. Even when outcomes remain uncertain, I exercise the muscle of hope — believing, envisioning, and preparing for what can be. My hope is not naive; it is rooted, grounded, and resilient.
"I choose hope as a discipline. My hope is strong, steady, and rooted in what is possible."

Chapter 15 – The Emotional Framework for Recovery

Recovery is more than logistics — it is emotional work. I honor the invisible weight carried by those I serve and by myself. Healing requires patience, presence, and emotional steadiness. My leadership holds space for grief and growth to coexist. I allow recovery to unfold without forcing its pace.
"I lead with emotional steadiness. I hold space for healing to emerge in its own time."

Chapter 16 – Leading Through Displacement

Displacement disrupts identity and belonging. I recognize the quiet losses hidden beneath physical relocation. My leadership becomes an anchor for those who have lost familiar ground. I offer stability, dignity, and compassion while helping others rebuild both externally and internally.
"I lead with compassion. I create safety and dignity for those who have lost their footing."

Chapter 17 – The Spirit of the Response

The way I lead matters as much as what I do. I carry the spirit of service, humility, and courage into every response. My leadership is not transactional — it is human. In every decision, I choose to lead with integrity that honors both the moment and the people within it. **"I lead with integrity and heart. My leadership serves both the moment and the person."**

Appendix I

Global Partnership & Coordination Checklist

Use this quick-reference guide when working with external NGOs, donors, government agencies, or international responders to ensure culturally respectful, emotionally intelligent, and sustainable partnerships.

1. **Establish Shared Purpose**
   - Have both parties clearly defined the purpose and scope of collaboration?
   - Are community needs driving the partnership, not external agendas?

2. **Respect Local Leadership**
   - Are local elders, faith leaders, educators, and cultural anchors actively included?
   - Has community intelligence been consulted before decisions are made?

3. **Clarify Roles and Boundaries**
   - Have decision-making roles been agreed upon transparently?
   - Are responsibilities clearly delegated to avoid duplication or power struggles?

4. **Prioritize Dignity and Inclusion**
   - Are services designed to protect the dignity of vulnerable groups?
   - Have considerations for gender, age, disability, and marginalized populations been addressed?

5. **Cultural and Spiritual Awareness**
   - Have cultural traditions, languages, and faith practices been honored in service delivery?
   - Have global partners received cultural briefings before entering the field?

6. **Emotional Safety for Staff and Community**
   - Are both responders and community members receiving emotional support where needed?
   - Are trauma-informed principles being applied throughout coordination efforts?

7. **Resource Transparency**
   - Have financial resources, supplies, and timelines been fully disclosed to all partners?
   - Are resource distributions being monitored for equity and fairness?

8. **Communication Protocols**
   - Is there a single communication chain to reduce confusion and misinformation?
   - Are language barriers addressed through trusted translators or cultural liaisons?

9. **Long-Term Sustainability**
   - Is the partnership building local capacity for leadership and recovery after external teams depart?
   - Are local leaders being empowered to maintain recovery systems independently?

10. **Conflict Resolution Pathways**
    - Have all partners agreed on how disagreements will be addressed respectfully?
    - Is there a mechanism for adjusting plans if unforeseen challenges arise?

How to Use This Checklist:

Leaders may use this as a discussion guide during initial planning meetings, partnership evaluations, or global field coordination sessions. It is intended to protect community dignity while fostering healthy collaboration between external agencies and local leadership.

Appendix J

Digital Grief Reflection Worksheet

Processing Emotional Overload from Global Crises

Even when you are not physically present at the scene of a disaster, your nervous system can still absorb emotional weight from what you witness through media, news coverage, and global events. Use this guided reflection to nurture your emotional center as you navigate digital exposure.

1. Identify the Event
What recent global or national event have you found yourself emotionally affected by?
(Describe briefly.)

2. Source of Exposure
How did you first learn about this event?

- € News coverage
- € Social media
- € Conversations with others
- € Live footage
- € Other

3. Emotional Response

What emotions surfaced for you while witnessing or learning about this event?

- € Grief
- € Helplessness
- € Fear
- € Anger
- € Guilt
- € Numbness
- € Compassion fatigue
- € Other

4. Signs of Emotional Overload

Have you noticed any signs of emotional fatigue or overload in your daily functioning?

- € Sleep disruption
- € Anxiety or worry
- € Emotional heaviness
- € Irritability
- € Feeling disconnected
- € Physical tension or discomfort
- € Other

5. Media Boundaries

What boundaries or media practices might help protect your emotional capacity going forward?
(List one or two specific adjustments you can make.)

6. Redirecting Compassion

Where can you redirect your care or compassion within your own community or sphere of influence?
(List one or two small, meaningful actions you can take.)

Closing Reflection

You are allowed to feel.
You are allowed to grieve.
You are also allowed to release what does not belong to you.

References & Resources

For further learning, context, and implementation

This book draws from a blend of psychological research, humanitarian fieldwork, crisis communication scholarship, and trauma-informed leadership practices. The following references and resources can guide deeper study and support implementation in various communities and global contexts.

Appendix K

Global Resource Index

Disaster Response, Leadership, and Emotional Recovery Tools

◈ Leadership & Recovery Frameworks

Sphere Handbook (Humanitarian Charter and Minimum Standards in Humanitarian Response)
A globally recognized set of principles and standards guiding humanitarian response in disasters.

Sendai Framework for Disaster Risk Reduction (UNDRR)
A 15-year global agreement outlining actions to reduce disaster risk and strengthen resilience.

Mosaic Intelligence Method™ (Dr. Karissa Thomas)
A leadership model that integrates emotional integrity, cultural flexibility, and identity agility to guide inclusive and adaptive leadership in crisis and recovery settings.

◈ Key Organizations to Know

UN OCHA – United Nations Office for the Coordination of Humanitarian Affairs
Coordinates international emergency response and ensures cohesive relief efforts.

IFRC – International Federation of Red Cross and Red Crescent Societies
Offers humanitarian aid, disaster preparedness, and community resilience support.

BRAC (Bangladesh)
One of the world's largest NGOs supporting development, education, and disaster relief.

Doctors Without Borders (MSF)
Provides rapid-response medical aid in crisis zones globally.

FEMA (United States)
Federal agency managing national disaster response and recovery.

NDMA (India) – National Disaster Management Authority
Coordinates India's disaster risk management and preparedness systems.

CADRE (Africa) – Center for African Disaster Risk Engagement
Develops localized strategies and leadership capacity for disaster risk reduction across the African continent.

◈ Training Tools & Resources

Psychological First Aid (PFA) Manual – WHO
A practical, scalable framework for providing emotional support in disaster settings.

Harvard Humanitarian Initiative
Offers research, training, and resources in disaster response and crisis leadership.

Emotional Intelligence Leadership Competency Model (Daniel Goleman)

A research-based model for cultivating emotionally intelligent leadership in high-stress and high-stakes environments.

Recommended Use

Use this resource index to:

- Train culturally responsive disaster leaders
- Support global volunteers and recovery workers
- Supplement classroom and field instruction
- Embed emotional resilience into technical training
- Bridge community knowledge with global recovery frameworks

Appendix L

Recovery Design Checklist (Do vs. Don't)

Do	Don't
Involve community voices in all stages of design	Assume technical experts know what the community needs
Preserve or create shared spaces for gathering, grieving, and storytelling	Focus only on housing or infrastructure without social cohesion
Use art, culture, and ceremony as part of the recovery process	Dismiss cultural or emotional rituals as non-essential
Plan for leadership transitions in trauma-informed care	Rely on a single point person or external agency for emotional support
Provide mental health resources that are culturally accessible	Use generic or outsourced services without local trust
Build recovery markers or memorials to honor collective loss	Avoid public recognition of grief and loss
Encourage intergenerational involvement in rebuilding	Prioritize speed over sustainability and inclusion

This checklist is designed to support governments, NGOs, educators, and community leaders in creating recovery environments that not only rebuild but restore.

Because when the invisible isn't designed for, it is often what lingers the longest.

Appendix M

Using This Book in Classrooms and Group Learning

Leading After the Storm is designed for broad, real-world impact. While it speaks directly to community leaders, educators, volunteers, adjusters, and everyday responders, it is also well-suited for structured group learning and university coursework.

This book has been used in academic and professional settings across disciplines including:

- Crisis leadership and emergency response
- Trauma-informed education
- Public administration and policy
- Global development and nonprofit leadership
- Mental health and resilience-building
- Cross-cultural communication and social work

Whether utilized in undergraduate courses, graduate seminars, leadership development programs, or NGO training cohorts, this book provides practical reflection prompts, narrative case examples, and modular chapters suitable for both discussion and self-paced application.

Suggested Use in Group or Academic Settings:

- Assign one chapter per session with journal reflection prompts as discussion openers
- Pair narrative vignettes with group case analysis or scenario planning
- Use "Framework in Action" boxes for leadership role-play or simulation
- Encourage learners to develop their own local crisis response tools using insights from the book

To support academic integration, an optional **Instructor Companion PDF** is available upon request, including:

- Discussion guides
- Writing prompts
- Suggested assignments
- Slide-friendly key takeaways

For access to instructor materials or speaking engagements, visit www.drkarissathomas.net or email: **drk@drkarissathomas.com**

Appendix N

Recovery Room Facilitator's Guide

Appendix to Leading After the Storm: How to Communicate, Calm, and Coordinate in the Wake of Disaster
By Dr. Karissa Thomas

Purpose of the Recovery Room

The Recovery Room is a dedicated space designed to support nervous system regulation, emotional decompression, and psychological restoration after collective or individual trauma. Whether used in a school, community center, workplace, or disaster recovery site, the room serves as a temporary sanctuary for reflection and resetting.

Your Role as Facilitator

You are not a therapist, counselor, or healer. You are a steady, emotionally aware guide who creates a safe space for others to process their experiences. Your tone, presence, and ability to model calm directly influence the effectiveness of this environment.

Setup Guidelines

- Create a quiet, low-stimulation environment
- Arrange seating in a circle or open cluster
- Dim overhead lighting and avoid harsh smells

- Provide grounding tools: soft blankets, tissues, natural textures
- Include printed prompts or anchor quotes from the book
- Play soft instrumental music, if culturally appropriate

Suggested Structure (30–60 minutes)

1. **Arrival and Grounding (5–10 mins)**
   Offer a shared breath, short silence, or anchor quote.

2. **Gentle Check-In (10 mins)**
   Ask: "What are you carrying today?" or "What does your body need right now?"

3. **Reflection Practice (10–20 mins)**
   Journaling, silent writing, or artistic expression encouraged. Use prompts such as:

   - "What are you holding that isn't yours to carry?"
   - "Where do you feel the storm in your body?"

4. **Regulation or Releasing (5–10 mins)**
   Offer breathwork, visualization, or a mindful walk.

5. **Closing (5–10 mins)**
   Invite one word or gesture to symbolize what they're taking with them. Close with a gentle reminder: "You are not alone."

Facilitator Do's and Don'ts

Do:

- Keep language clear, steady, and sparse
- Allow silence without rushing to fill it
- Use inclusive, culturally respectful practices
- Offer presence, not solutions
- Validate nonverbal processing

Don't:

- Force anyone to speak
- Treat the space as therapy
- Assume emotional responses will look the same
- Create rigid agendas or timelines
- Use emotionally triggering media or visuals

Optional Enhancements

- Recovery Reflection Cards with quotes from each chapter
- Journals with prompts for after-room processing
- Anchor Object Table (rocks, beads, wood, shells)
- A quiet wall or board for anonymous reflections

Best Chapters for Integration:

- *Chapter 6: Emotional Attunement* – supports group rhythm and silence
- *Chapter 12: The Leader's Survival Plan* – guides facilitator self-care
- *Chapter 15: Designing Recovery Spaces* – informs layout and emotional design

Reminder

The Recovery Room is not about fixing anyone. It is about presence, permission, and pacing. Your steadiness is the healing. The space does not require perfection—only care.

Key References

Emotional Intelligence & Leadership

1. Goleman, D. (1995). *Emotional Intelligence: Why It Can Matter More Than IQ.* Bantam.
2. Boyatzis, R., & McKee, A. (2005). *Resonant Leadership: Renewing Yourself and Connecting with Others Through Mindfulness, Hope, and Compassion.* Harvard Business Review Press.
3. Thomas, K. (2025). *The Mosaic Intelligence Method*™. [forthcoming]

Crisis, Trauma, and Disaster Recovery

4. Herman, J. (1997). *Trauma and Recovery.* Basic Books.
5. van der Kolk, B. (2014). *The Body Keeps the Score: Brain, Mind, and Body in the Healing of Trauma.* Penguin Books.
6. Everly, G. S., & Lating, J. M. (2013). *A Clinical Guide to the Treatment of the Human Stress Response.* Springer.

Cross-Cultural and Global Humanitarian Contexts

7. Sphere Association. (2018). *The Sphere Handbook: Humanitarian Charter and Minimum Standards in Humanitarian Response.* www.spherestandards.org
8. Inter-Agency Standing Committee (IASC). (2007). *Guidelines on Mental Health and Psychosocial Support in Emergency Settings.* www.who.int
9. Heifetz, R., Grashow, A., & Linsky, M. (2009). *The Practice of Adaptive Leadership: Tools and Tactics for Changing Your Organization and the World.* Harvard Business Press.

Toolkits and Field Manuals

10. International Federation of Red Cross and Red Crescent Societies. *Community Engagement and Accountability Toolkit.* www.ifrc.org
11. UNICEF. *Psychosocial Support for Children in Emergencies.* www.unicef.org
12. Harvard Humanitarian Initiative. *Signal Code: Ethical Obligations for Humanitarian Information Activities.* https://hhi.harvard.edu/

Recommended Reading for Practitioners

13. Wheatley, M. (2007). *Finding Our Way: Leadership for an Uncertain Time.* Berrett-Koehler.
14. Brown, B. (2018). *Dare to Lead: Brave Work. Tough Conversations. Whole Hearts.* Random House.
15. Weick, K., & Sutcliffe, K. (2007). *Managing the Unexpected: Resilient Performance in an Age of Uncertainty.* Wiley.

Global Training and Resource Organizations

16. **ReliefWeb** (www.reliefweb.int) – Global updates and training for humanitarian crises
17. **ALNAP** (www.alnap.org) – Evaluation and learning for humanitarian action
18. **Mental Health Innovation Network** (www.mhinnovation.net) – Global mental health solutions for underserved regions
19. **CrisisReady** (Harvard T.H. Chan School of Public Health) – Decision-making frameworks for public health emergencies

If you are using this book for professional development, training, or cross-sector collaboration, please cite accordingly and explore the partner tools available through *The Mosaic Way*™ and *Efficient Adjuster*™.

For licensing, bulk training orders, or speaker engagements, visit: **www.drkarissathomas.net**

About the Author

Dr. Karissa Thomas is a global leadership strategist, award-winning author, and creator of The Mosaic Intelligence Method™—a transformative framework equipping leaders to navigate emotional complexity, cultural nuance, and identity shifts in high-stakes environments.

With more than two decades of cross-sector experience—including corporate leadership, international education, crisis recovery, and humanitarian training—Dr. Thomas brings a uniquely human perspective to systems change. Her work spans the United States, the Middle East, Africa, Southeast Asia, and the Caribbean, where she has supported frontline professionals, educators, and NGO teams navigating the emotional and structural realities of recovery.

As founder of Lady K Solutions, LLC, Efficient Adjuster™, and The Mosaic Way™, she empowers individuals and institutions to lead with clarity, care, and cultural responsiveness in moments of disruption. Her books and training programs are used globally across ministries, schools, leadership academies, and disaster response networks.

She holds a Doctorate in Educational Leadership and an Executive MBA, and continues to teach and train thousands of learners worldwide on the intersection of compassion, crisis, and cross-cultural leadership.

Dr. Thomas believes the future of recovery depends not only on operational systems, but on the emotional depth and relational integrity of those trusted to lead others through the unknown.

For global consulting, leadership training, or licensing inquiries, visit: www.drkarissathomas.net or contact drk@drkarissathomas.com

Afterword: A World Still Stirring

Global Watch – Geological Unrest in 2025

Though this book centers on storms, floods, and systemic upheaval, the Earth continues to speak in many forms.

As of mid-2025, Alaska's Mount Spurr remains under close observation for volcanic unrest. Elevated seismic activity, ground deformation, and gas emissions signal that the region may face more than just cold and snow—it may soon face ash, air disruptions, and sudden evacuations. In Hawaii, Kīlauea's lava-fountaining paused briefly in July, only to show signs of reawakening beneath the summit.

No major eruptions have occurred at the time of this writing. But that's the nature of preparedness. It isn't just about what has already come—it's about how we lead when the ground begins to shift, when visibility fades, and when clarity must come from within.

Whether you're navigating hurricanes, heatwaves, wildfires, or the tremors beneath your feet, the core leadership tools remain the same:
Calm. Communication. Coordination. And Care.

If there is one lasting message to carry forward, it is this:
Even when the storm passes, the responsibility to lead—emotionally, relationally, and structurally—remains. The world will stir again.
And when it does, so will you.
With strength. With clarity. With others.